CARIBBEAN COMPETITIVENESS THROUGH GLOBAL VALUE CHAINS

CARIBBEAN COMPETITIVENESS THROUGH GLOBAL VALUE CHAINS

EDITED BY **INDERA SAGEWAN-ALLI**

THE UNIVERSITY OF THE WEST INDIES PRESS
Jamaica • Barbados • Trinidad and Tobago

The Caribbean Centre for Competitiveness
The University of the West Indies, St Augustine Campus

The University of the West Indies Press
7A Gibraltar Hall Road, Mona
Kingston 7, Jamaica
www.uwipress.com
and
The Caribbean Centre for Competitiveness
The University of the West Indies, St Augustine Campus
Trinidad and Tobago

© The Caribbean Centre for Competitiveness, 2016
All rights reserved. Published 2016

A catalogue record of this book is available from the National Library of Jamaica.

ISBN: 978-976-640-603-5 (print)
       978-976-640-604-2 (Kindle)
       978-976-640-605-9 (ePub)

Cover design by Robert Harris
Typesetting by The Beget, India
Printed in the United States of America

The University of the West Indies Press has no responsibility for the persistence or accuracy of URLs for external or third-party Internet websites referred to in this publication and does not guarantee that any content on such websites is, or will remain accurate or appropriate.

Contents

List of Figures	ix
List of Tables	xi
Acknowledgements	xiii
Abbreviations	xv
Introduction	1
Indera Sagewan-Alli	

Section 1. Manufacturing Industry Case Studies

Case Study 1. A St Lucian Experience for Sustainable Participation in the Agro-Foods Global Value Chain: The Case of Baron Foods Limited — 17

Vimlawatti St Hill and Jacintha Lee

1.1	Introduction	17
1.2	The Global Condiment, Sauces, Dressings and Seasonings Market	19
1.3	Baron Foods' Participation in the Condiments and Sauces Global Value Chain	21
1.4	Key Elements Driving Baron Foods' Export Success	21
1.5	Local Industry Conditions: Challenges for Other Firms	25
1.6	Lessons Learned	29
1.7	Policy Recommendations for Sector Development	29

Case Study 2. A Structural Analysis of the Competitiveness of the Hot Pepper Sauce Industry in Trinidad and Tobago: A Global Value Chain Approach   39

Shellyanne Wilson

2.1	Introduction	40
2.2	The Hot Pepper Sauce Global Value Chain	40
2.3	Hot Pepper Production	41
2.4	Hot Pepper Paste/Mash Production	42
2.5	Hot Pepper Sauce Production	42
2.6	Overview of the Hot Pepper Sauce Industry in Trinidad and Tobago	44
2.7	Actors in Trinidad and Tobago's Value Chain	44
2.8	Local Industry Conditions	50
2.9	Firm Strategy, Structure and Rivalry	51
2.10	Related and Supporting Institutions	51
2.11	Lessons Learned	52
2.12	Upgrading Strategies for the Local Hot Pepper Sauce Industry	53
2.13	Recommendations	55
2.14	Conclusion	56

Case Study 3. The Rum Industry of Guyana in the Global Value Chain   61

Dianna DaSilva-Glasgow and Louis Dodson

3.1	Introduction	61
3.2	Input-Output Structure of the Rum Global Value Chain	62
3.3	Rum Production	64
3.4	Blending	65
3.5	Bottling	65
3.6	Distribution	65
3.7	Global Supply and Demand for Rum	66
3.8	Market Segments	71
3.9	Global Trends	71
3.10	Assessing Guyana's Participation in the Rum Global Value Chain	74
3.11	Production and Export Trends	76

3.12 Analysis of Factors Affecting Guyana's Competitiveness	78
3.13 Role of Key Stakeholders in Guyana's Rum Industry	81
3.14 Upgrading Strategies and Tactics	81
3.15 SWOT Analysis of Guyana's Rum Industry	85
3.16 Lessons Learned	86
3.17 Recommendations for Further Upgrading	87
3.18 Policy Recommendation	88
3.19 Conclusion	89

Case Study 4. VincyFresh Limited: A Caribbean Case Study on Export Competitiveness and Global Value Chain Analysis — 93

Heidi E. Vincent and Simone N. Murray

4.1 Introduction	93
4.2 The Global Fruit and Vegetable Processing Industry	94
4.3 VincyFresh in the Fruit and Vegetable Global Value Chain	99
4.4 The Fruit and Vegetable Processing Industry in St Vincent and the Grenadines	101
4.5 Factors Affecting St Vincent and the Grenadines' Competitiveness in the Food-Processing Sector	105
4.6 Lessons Learned	112
4.7 Upgrading Recommendations for VincyFresh	113

Section 2. Services Industry Case Studies

Case Study 5. The Chaguaramas Ship Repair Cluster: Sustaining Competitiveness and Lessons for Upgrading along the Maritime Value Chain — 127

Don Charles, Debbie A. Mohammed and Preeya Mohan

5.1 Introduction	128
5.2 Overview of the Chaguaramas Cluster	128
5.3 The Global Ship Repair Industry	130
5.4 The Regional Ship Repair Industry	131
5.5 The Ship Repair Global Value Chain	132

5.6	Local Competitiveness Factors	135
5.7	Lessons Learned	140
5.8	Upgrading Strategies	141
5.9	Recommendations	143
5.10	Conclusion	147

Case Study 6. The Future of Solar Water Heaters in Barbados: Market Expansion or Product Innovation? — 151

Andrea N. Baldwin and Olivia Chase-Smith

6.1	Introduction	152
6.2	The Solar Water Heating System and the Global Value Chain	153
6.3	Solar Water Heaters: A Global Perspective	153
6.4	Overview of the Local Solar Water Heating Industry in Barbados	157
6.5	Support for the Solar Water Heating Industry	160
6.6	Local Industry Conditions	161
6.7	Factor Conditions	163
6.8	Firm Strategies	164
6.9	Lessons Learned	164
6.10	Recommended Strategies	166

Figures

1.1.	Baron Foods' participation in the condiments and sauces global value chain	22
2.1.	Global value chain for the hot pepper sauce industry	41
3.1.	Input-output structure of the rum global value chain	63
3.2.	Top fifteen exporters of rum, 2005–2012	72
3.3.	Top fifteen importers of rum, 2005–2012	73
3.4.	Guyana's participation in the rum global value chain	74
3.5.	Guyana's rum production (thousands of litres)	76
3.6.	Guyana's rum exports by major destinations (US$ millions)	77
3.7.	Guyana's exports of bulk and bottled rum to the EU25	77
4.1.	VincyFresh within the fruit and vegetable global value chain	95
5.1.	Key companies of the Chaguaramas ship repair cluster	130
5.2.	Ship repair global value chain	133
5.3.	Trinidad and Tobago's ship repair value chain	134
5.4.	Overview of main activities of Trinidad and Tobago's ship repair industry	135
5.5.	Comparative and competitive advantages of Trinidad and Tobago's ship repair industry	138
5.6.	SWOT analysis of Trinidad and Tobago's ship repair industry	141
6.1.	Solar water heater global value chain	154
6.2.	Imports and exports of solar water heaters in Barbados, 2008–2012	162

Tables

1.1.	Comparative Export Data: Condiments and Sauces (US$ millions)	19
1.2.	Baron Foods' Local Sales and Exports, 2000–2012	20
1.3.	Competition in the St Lucia Condiment and Sauces Market	20
1.4.	SWOT Analysis of Baron Foods	26
1.5.	Factors Affecting St Lucia's Competitiveness in the Agro-Processing Global Value Chain	27
1.6.	Lessons Learned from Baron Foods' Evolution as an Exporter	30
2.1.	Lead Firms by Parent Industry and by Market	43
2.2.	Characteristics of Hot Pepper Sauce Processors	46
3.1.	Top Five Best-Selling Global Rum Brands, 2011	64
3.2.	Leading Rum Producers Worldwide, 2014	67
3.3.	Top Ten Rum Brands in Europe ('000s of 9-litre cases)	68
3.4.	Investments by Key Rum-Producing Firms	70
3.5.	Market Segment in which Major Firms Operate	72
3.6.	Subsidiaries and Associates of Demerara Distillers Limited	75
3.7.	Key Stakeholders in the Guyana Rum Industry	82
3.8.	Guyana's Rum Industry Upgrading Strategies	84
3.9.	Upgrading Tactics of the Firms in Guyana's Rum Industry	84
3.10.	SWOT Analysis of Guyana's Rum Industry	85
4.1.	Lead Firms in the Fruit and Vegetable Processing Industry	96
4.2.	Lead Exporters and Importers in the Fruit and Vegetable Processing Industry	97
4.3.	VincyFresh Product Lines and Ranges	99
4.4.	VincyFresh Export Statistics	101
4.5.	SWOT Analysis of the Agro-Processing Industry in St Vincent and the Grenadines	103
4.6.	Factors Affecting St Vincent and the Grenadines' Competitiveness (Part 1)	108
4.7.	Current Trade Agreements	110

4.8.	Factors Affecting St Vincent and the Grenadines' Competitiveness (Part 2)	111
5.1.	Number of Docks in the Caribbean That Can Accommodate Vessels Larger Than 300 Metres	132
6.1.	Domestic Firms in the Solar Water Heating Sector in Barbados	158
6.2.	Fiscal Incentives to Stimulate the Solar Water Heating Sector in Barbados	160
6.3.	Barbados National Standards Applied to Solar Water Heaters and Renewable Energy	163
6.4.	Upgrading Strategies, Potential Barriers and Business Model Proposals for the Solar Water Heating Industry in Barbados	167

Acknowledgements

The publication of this book satisfies a deliverable of the Caribbean Centre for Competitiveness under the technical agreement arrangement with its donors – the Inter-American Development Bank and the United Kingdom Department for International Development. The Caribbean Centre for Competitiveness is therefore grateful to both these institutions for providing funding for technical capacity-building towards developing knowledge products such as this which can contribute to improving the competitiveness of Caribbean firms and industries.

Sincerest appreciations to Gary Gereffi, Penny Bamber and Karina Fernandez-Stark of Duke University's Center on Globalization, Governance and Competitiveness for training case writers across the Caribbean region in global value chain analysis methodology.

Thanks to all the authors for their hard and professional work, in particular Dianna DaSilva-Glasgow for additional research and administrative support.

Acknowledgements to company and industry representatives and public officials who participated in interviews, provided relevant statistics and made relevant policy documents available to researchers.

Kamlini Dalipsingh is singled out for special recognition for her unwavering commitment to bringing this project to its successful completion, extending beyond the call of duty to work through time-consuming glitches.

Finally, thanks to the University of the West Indies for providing the institutional space for the Caribbean Centre for Competitiveness to have developed into a regional centre of excellence in competitiveness.

Abbreviations

BFL	Baron Foods Limited
CARICOM	Caribbean Community
DDL	Demerara Distillers Limited
GVC	global value chain
LNG	liquefied natural gas
PV	photovoltaic
SWH	solar water heating
SWHs	solar water heaters
SWOT	strengths weaknesses opportunities threats
WIRSPA	West Indies Rum and Spirits Association
WTO	World Trade Organization

Introduction

INDERA SAGEWAN-ALLI

Background

Firms and industries worldwide do not operate in isolation; they are all part of a global chain of production and value adding which is becoming more and more fragmented. The OECD (2013) argues that global "value chains have become a dominant feature of the world economy". Countries at all levels of development are involved, from the poorest to the most advanced. The production of goods and services increasingly occurs wherever the necessary skills and materials are available at competitive cost and quality.

The analytical approach of value chain analysis is focused on understanding how global industries are organized by examining the structure and dynamics of different actors involved in the particular sector (Gereffi and Fernandez-Stark 2011). It undertakes a firm-level or sector analysis and focuses on the sequence of value added within an industry from conception and production to end use, to determine the value added of each component (Gereffi and Fernandez-Stark 2011). Global value chain (GVC) analysis traces the patterns of global production over time and links the industry's geographically dispersed activities and actors in developed and developing countries. In so doing, it can also provide a basis for sound corporate and industry strategizing towards improved and sustained competiveness and growth.

UNCTAD (2013) offers a number of illustrative points regarding the transformations that GVCs have brought to world trade:

1. Trade and investment are inextricably intertwined and are shaped by transnational corporations through transnational production networks.
2. Developing countries are increasingly participating in GVCs and presently account for over 40 per cent of value-added trade with their participation being led by foreign direct investments through transnational corporations.
3. There are a number of GVC development paths including "engaging", "upgrading", "leapfrogging" and "competing" via GVC with increasing participation and upgrading offering the best development outcomes for developing countries.

The concept of upgrading captures the movement from lower to higher value-added activities and services in the chain where competiveness can improve with other socio-economic multiplier effects such as employment creation, foreign direct investment, rural development, human skills development and economic growth[1] and resilience.

Objectives

In the competitiveness literature, there is a dearth of analytical material on Caribbean firms. Therefore, the main objective of this book is to contribute to filling this gap through the compilation of firm and industry case studies on the Caribbean region utilizing the research methodological approach of GVC analysis. Another objective is to broadly contribute to the development of policies that can augment the competitiveness of the firms/industries in the global economy and provide lessons for other firms to emulate. The studies are meant to provide an understanding of the firms/industries under study as they operate within the GVC. They explore the strategies used by these selected firms/industries to attain competitiveness in the context of the global market, the strategies of leading global firms, the governance of the global market, the structure and functioning of the local policy and institutional environment for business and how value is created, all for the purpose of identifying areas where upgrading at the local firm/industry level can take place and so increase the local value capture either by firm, industry or country.

Methodology

This book is the outcome of a special project of the Caribbean Centre for Competitiveness aimed at producing original value chain studies on Caribbean firms and productive sectors. It involved the training of the respective researchers and authors from across the Caribbean in the value chain methodology, followed by the use of this analytical tool to conduct the research. The training was conducted by the Duke University Center on Globalization, Governance and Competitiveness.

The analytical value chain methodology offers a holistic approach to the study of global industries by detailing input-output structures, geographical scope, governance structure and institutional context in which the industry's value chain is embedded (Gereffi 1995). The input-output structure maps all the activities necessary to bring the product or service from conception to the consumer, including research and design, inputs, production, distribution and marketing, sales, and in some cases the recycling of products after use. It traces the evolution of the industry and the trends that have shaped its organization in order to identify the various segments of the chain which add value to create the product. The geographical analysis identifies the lead firms in each segment of the value chain through firm data, specialized industry reports and interviews with industry experts to determine the country's position within the GVC. Studying industry exports and the segments in which those exports are concentrated provides the basis for analysing the possibilities for shifting geographic scope of the industry. Industry governance, defined by Gereffi (1995) as the "authority and power relationships that determine how financial, material and human resources are allocated and flow within a chain" provides an understanding of how a chain is controlled and coordinated. This is important as it facilitates entry into and development of the industry. Further, analysis of the institutional framework identifies how local, national and international conditions and policies shape the GVC and can be developed and leveraged for improved competitiveness.

GVC analysis uses a bottom-up approach in which stakeholder analysis through interview plays a critical role. Therefore, researchers collected data through interviews, site visits and the compilation of secondary published statistics. Using the methodological approach, data collection, analysis and presentation of findings are inextricably linked. As such, the studies all follow a common format which includes an analysis of the global industry, the local industry and recommendations for upgrading in the global market.

Summary of Cases

The GVC cases presented in this publication provide firm and sector/industry level analyses. They broadly cover manufacturing and service industries with an emphasis on manufacturing and agro-processing in particular. As such, the book is structured into two sections. The first section provides four case studies in the manufacturing industry: (1) agro-foods, through the experience of Baron Foods Limited (BFL) in St Lucia; (2) VincyFresh in St Vincent and the Grenadines; (3) the hot pepper sauce industry in Trinidad and Tobago; and (4) beverages, through the experience of the rum industry in Guyana. The second part provides two case studies in the services industry: (1) the Chaguaramas ship repair cluster in Trinidad and Tobago; and (2) the solar water heating industry in Barbados.

Case 1 is "A St Lucian Experience for Sustainable Participation in the Agro-Foods Global Value Chain: The Case of Baron Foods Limited". BFL accounts for a significant share of St Lucia's exports in condiments and sauces. Although the Caribbean region is not a major exporter of these commodities, comparative data indicates that the global percentage share of exports from St Lucia has increased every year from 2006 to 2010, with the exception of 2009. Productivity, innovation, flexibility and responsiveness to consumers have been critical guiding principles of BFL's value chain. BFL maximizes its value within the chain by identifying niche product opportunities in major markets and ensuring strong coordination throughout the supply chain. BFL has leveraged key opportunities to add value to its products through process, product and functional upgrading. There are three factors that stand out in BFL's history as being important for its upgrading success:

1. It has actively pursued certification and focused on producing high-quality products that meet the tastes of consumers.
2. It has ensured that its workforce is constantly trained sufficiently in order to maintain the company's quality standards.
3. BFL has made its company an attractive place to work to ensure a sustainable workforce.

For its raw materials, BFL has tapped upstream into the agro-producing sector primarily through an outgrower programme (contract farming). Among the challenges being experienced are limited availability of appropriate skills, inconsistency of quality and supply of raw materials, and weak coordination among policy and service entities. These challenges could be addressed through the provision of relevant education and training activities at various levels in the agro-processing system and the effective coordination of the sector through the strengthening of linkages among the relevant stakeholders along the value chain, in particular within the agriculture industry.

The second case is "A Structural Analysis of the Competitiveness of the Hot Pepper Sauce Industry in Trinidad and Tobago: A Global Value Chain Approach". The hot pepper–producing countries are concentrated in Asia, South and Central America, and Africa because of climatic conditions that are suitable for the growing of hot peppers and also to lower labour costs. In the Western Hemisphere, Mexico, Columbia, Costa Rica and Ecuador are the most prominent producers of pepper mash. Globally, the companies that concentrate on hot pepper sauce production vary by size and product focus. The Tabasco brand of the McIlhenny Company is considered to be the global leader in the hot pepper sauce industry. There are large food multinational corporations entering the "fiery foods" segment, where spicy ingredients are incorporated into food items, such as snack foods and condiments. For example, Heinz introduced a range of hot sauces in 2012. The hot pepper industry is a relatively small but growing segment of the overall food and beverage processing sector – its estimated value was US$15.6 million in 2012.

The Trinidad and Tobago hot pepper sauce industry comprises actors that span the full range of value chain activities, from hot pepper research and development, through hot pepper cultivation and harvesting, pepper mash and hot pepper sauce production, to sales and distribution of various products. While the industry has major players in the condiments, sauces and dressings segment of the local and CARICOM food industry, the Trinidad and Tobago hot pepper sauce industry does not have any lead firms or major players at the global level. Despite its limited global presence, the local industry is vibrant, ranging from micro-processors to large food processors. These processors have leveraged Trinidad and Tobago's indigenous pepper varieties, such as the Trinidad Moruga Scorpion, to create a range of product offerings that meet the palette of the customer who enjoys spicy and fiery foods. Additionally, the processors have experimented with different flavourings such as rum, mango and tamarind to produce specialty pepper sauces. Many of the processors also have an online presence, using their own websites, specialty hot sauce websites and social media to market their product offerings globally.

The global spicy foods markets are also evolving by incorporating hot sauces into a variety of traditional products, as seen with Heinz's introduction of chilli sauces, and the collaboration between Unilever and Frank's Red Hot in the production of a spicy form of mayonnaise. At least two major challenges to growth were identified in the value chain analysis of the Trinidad and Tobago hot pepper sauce industry:

1. There is insufficient local supply of hot peppers. To alleviate the shortages, a revitalization of the agricultural sector is needed, including expansion of existing agricultural incentives and commercial farming programmes to include hot peppers.
2. In terms of local industry structure, there is little coordination between upstream and downstream segments of the value chain. The establishment of cooperatives for hot pepper farmers and the use of contractual arrangements for supplying hot peppers to the pepper mash and hot pepper sauce processors could improve the reliability of supply, thereby allowing the industry actors to engage in upgrading activities.

The third case is "The Rum Industry of Guyana in the Global Value Chain". The Caribbean and Latin America are regarded as the epicentre of global rum production. There is a pre-eminence of multinational corporations, mostly based in developed countries but with operations and partnerships that span developing countries, particularly in the premium end of the market. For instance, British multinational alcoholic beverage company Diageo, headquartered in London, operates twenty-seven production facilities, including distillation and bottling facilities in Scotland, Italy, France, Spain, Germany, England, Puerto Rico and Mexico, among others. The companies that are leading suppliers of rum globally have been successful by implementing a number of strategies, including branding, vertically integrating operations along the value chain, outsourcing, investing in multiple strategic markets and differentiating production techniques.

Guyana operates along the full spectrum of the global rum value chain from sugar production to marketing and distribution. It mainly exports bulk and branded rum to Europe and the United States. Guyana's success, however, has been in the premium niche market with aged dark rums produced and marketed by Demerara Distillers Limited under its flagship brand, El Dorado. The success of the company and of the rum-producing industry is linked to business specific investments as well as general improvements in the macroeconomic and business environment in Guyana. Trade policy plays a crucial role in investment, providing Guyana with preferential access to markets in the European

Union and the United States through the Lomé I agreement and the Caribbean Basin Economic Recovery Act. As it relates to investments, the Demerara Distillers Limited's business model, similar to that of its global competitors, strengthens its capacity to control most critical elements of the value chain by

- investing in professional skills and productive capacity;
- establishing company-owned commercial banks to ensure access to finance;
- becoming energy self-sufficient and improving marketing by establishing subsidiary operations in key export markets; and
- improving global visibility by participating in international wine and spirits competitions.

The key challenges presently confronting the industry, however, are the use of protectionist policies by governments in importing markets (such as subsidies in the United States which require policy advocacy at the governmental level for resolution), the state of the domestic sugar industry and the unreliable shipping infrastructure of the country. Resolving the latter of the two challenges requires improving the productive capacity of the sugar industry and the creation of a deep-water harbour.

The fourth case is "VincyFresh Limited: A Caribbean Case Study on Export Competitiveness and Global Value Chain Analysis". VincyFresh is the key lead firm in the fruit and vegetable processing industry in St Vincent and the Grenadines. Globally, the market is dominated by mass merchants and brand manufacturers. Mass merchants are large department or discount stores such as Walmart, Costco and Target, each carrying their own private label. Companies that have their own brand name as well as manufacturers such as Del Monte, Heinz and others are referred to as brand manufacturers. These lead firms generally acquire raw materials from contract growers who grow specific varieties of plants according to the processor requirements. Supply contracts generally run for one to ten years. Long-term contracts are generally negotiated by growers who would have to plant to fulfil the need of certain manufacturers but not see returns for several years. When growers and manufacturers enter into long-term contracts, price is often negotiated on an annual basis.

VincyFresh is involved in only two stages of the five-stage GVC of the fruit and vegetable industry – processing and packaging, and storage. The business model was chosen based on the demand from the diaspora for local fruit juices and vegetables. Growth in this sector is fuelled by a strong global demand for unprocessed agricultural products from the health and wellness sector. The main suppliers for St Vincent and the Grenadines' fruit and vegetable processing industry are farmers and vendors. Farmers serve the supply chain by providing produce to supermarkets, vendors, agro-processors, traders, institutions and the general population. While the supply of produce is one of the challenges facing the fruit and vegetable processing industry in the country, there are also opportunities, like the strong demand that exists for niche agricultural products like dasheen (also called taro) and expansion into other regional markets through the CARICOM Single Market and Economy. In response to the challenges, the government has partnered with the Food and Agriculture Organization and the Taiwan International Cooperation and Development Fund to establish a framework for development assistance. Productive capacity is another constraining factor for the sector: the minimum wage for unskilled industrial workers in St Vincent and the Grenadines is currently higher than regional competitor countries. Infrastructure and services – sea transportation to neighbouring islands other than Trinidad and Tobago or Barbados – are unreliable, which increases the challenge of maximizing the regional market. The country's business environment is another hindrance to development, with the World Bank ranking it 129 out of 185 global economies for the ease of getting credit. Growth in this segment of the value chain required revitalization of the upstream aspect, agricultural production and strengthening downstream in the sea transportation segment of the chain.

The fifth case is "The Chaguaramas Ship Repair Cluster: Sustaining Competitiveness and Lessons for Upgrading along the Maritime Value Chain". The major focus of ship repair activity is located in Chaguaramas, a harbour located in the north-western peninsula of Trinidad. Globally the ship repair cluster is dominated by countries in Europe, which collectively control approximately 35 per cent of world sales. Other major players in the global industry include China, India, Japan, Dubai and Singapore. Although Trinidad and Tobago is a very small player in the global ship repair industry, capturing less than 1 per cent of global sales, the potential for increasing its share of the regional ship repair value chain is promising, owing to

- proximity to the Americas and the Panama Canal, which allows Trinidad and Tobago to benefit from north-south and south-south trade;
- a highly developed hydrocarbon industry, which creates jobs for the ship repair cluster;
- favourable taxation rates;

- bilateral trade agreements with several Central and South American countries; and
- a cadre of specialized labour in its maritime industry.

The most important drivers of growth for Trinidad and Tobago have been its close proximity to the Americas and a growing downstream energy sector.

Trinidad and Tobago currently has four large companies and numerous small service companies operating in ship repair GVC, although its position is relatively insignificant when compared to large players such as Singapore, South Korea, China, Japan and countries in Europe. The ship repair industry contributes an estimated US$17 million (approximately 1 per cent) annually to the country's gross domestic product and creates more than 350 direct jobs (0.05 per cent of the labour force). Two main challenges impeding Trinidad and Tobago's ship repair industry growth are availability and reliability of skilled labour supply, and product upgrading. The labour challenge can be addressed by increasing the amount of maritime-related technical training programmes at Trinidad and Tobago's tertiary education institutions. The product upgrading challenge can be addressed through strategic partnerships with international yards which can facilitate the transfer of operational processes, technologies and efficiencies. These strategies may allow the Trinidad and Tobago ship repair cluster to upgrade into additional segments of the maritime GVC.

The sixth case is "The Future of Solar Water Heaters in Barbados: Market Expansion or Product Innovation?" Globally, each stage of the value chain is dominated by a few major players. The largest firms are starting to integrate vertically to cover all stages of manufacturing. In 2007, China's exports of solar water heaters grew by 28 per cent to US$65 million. In 2011, China led the world in solar thermal glazed installations, accounting for an estimated 58 per cent of global capacity, with Europe a distant second. While Chinese firms export to approximately fifty countries and territories in Europe, the United States and Southeast Asia, an important share of exports go to developing countries in Africa and Central and South America. The ability of Chinese firms to produce solar water heaters and lead the industry is partly based on government subsidies. Europe remains a key player in the industry in terms of both demand and supply.

The solar water heating sector in Barbados emerged as an alternative energy solution for the production of hot water for local domestic and commercial use. All firms in the sector engage all elements of its GVC – materials, components, manufacture, sales, installation and after-sales service. Value improvements in the solar water heating sector in Barbados continue to be driven by improvements in the application of technology, product research to improve the functionality, longevity and appearance of successive units, and of course market share – although at a slow pace.

For many years, sector growth was mostly driven by government support in the form of policy incentives aimed at boosting domestic and regional growth. In addition, the industry collectively sought to improve the value of its product through the use of new or improved materials and components, competitively enhancing finished quality and performance, sales and distribution strategies, and after-sales service. The sector has reached maturity in terms of its current business cycle. It must therefore pursue several vertical upgrading strategies to extract other sources of revenue and secure a global standard of competitiveness. These include intensifying its efforts to source funds for research and development, securing investment in upgraded technology, and pursuing strategic partnerships through forward linkages with value-added research and development firms or with companies offering contemporary renewable energy solutions that can maximize the possibilities for competing in the market.

Summary of Key Findings and Policy Implications

The overarching finding emanating from these studies is that sustained company and industry growth depends on finding ways to increase value-creating propositions. With respect to all four agro-processing cases, the weaknesses in the local raw material supply link of the chain stand out as major constraints. Since these economies are traditionally producers and exporters of primary products such as sugar in the case of Guyana, fresh peppers in Trinidad and Tobago, and fresh fruit and vegetables in St Vincent, the processing stage is an attempt at increasing the value retention to the respective countries. The challenge is to sustainably develop the primary production element of the value chain such that a reliable and cost efficient source of input can be fed into processing so that this second stage too can continually expand.

All the studies revealed that value-added processing continues to be dominated by developed countries which import raw agricultural products (largely from developing countries) at very low prices, then process and re-export at significantly higher values. Strengthening the local supply of raw materials provides a more competitive positioning of these industries globally. The BFL outgrower contractual model with farmers appears to be an efficient one which can be duplicated by the pepper sauce industry in Trinidad and Tobago and VincyFresh in St Vincent. This can result in a win-win situation wherein farmers engage in higher productivity-driven agricultural practices (thus increasing their respective incomes), while industry gets the supply it needs to access higher-value markets. It must be noted that even though the BFL contract model with farmers has been largely successful, it still suffers from inconsistency in the quality and supply of raw materials. The state could therefore play a significant role in strengthening its technical and financial support to farmers.

The dominance of developed country firms is also evident in the cases that are not agro-based – solar energy and ship repair. In the case of the former, the global industry is monopolized by European and Chinese manufacturers. The local industry evolved largely in response to government policy through an attractive incentive scheme to household users of solar-generated heaters. Given the small size of the Barbadian market, this industry has now exhausted the benefits to be derived from this scheme and must be creative in its growth plan or face stagnation.

The ship repair industry in Trinidad and Tobago emerged in response to emergency ship repair needs, largely because of the country's prime shipping route location. Though long in existence, it is yet to be recognized in the global industry as a ship repair hub; and for local industries to grow along the value chain, rationalization of purpose and potential is needed.

In the case of solar energy, the recommendation emerging is that the industry needs to engage in research and development towards new product development, and with respect to ship repair, a clearly defined strategy, investment in new technology, marketing and human resource development is needed. A cluster approach that brings together and harnesses the capabilities of all stakeholders would be useful in developing this industry.

Another important finding is the opportunity for niche positioning so that premium prices can be attained. This is highlighted in both the pepper sauce and rum cases. In the case of pepper sauce, the global lead suppliers are increasingly moving into specialty flavoured pepper sauces, and in the case of rum, although Guyana is largely an exporter of bulk rum, the evidence suggests that there are significantly higher margins in the production of premium high-quality rums. Given the availability of a variety of pepper flavours and potential fruit additives available in Trinidad and Tobago, Guyana and indeed the Caribbean region, there are opportunities to differentiate on premium pepper and rum flavours – allowing both industries to potentially expand along the value chain, capturing greater value.

This implies that focused research into optimizing the special and differentiated qualities of tropical peppers, molasses, fruits and vegetables can further enhance prospects for adding value along the production chain. Herein lies a role for research institutions such as the University of the West Indies, the Caribbean Industrial Research Institute and the Caribbean Agricultural Research and Development Institute in support of such initiatives. An important role for policy also emerges, as the state, through its incentive programmes, can create product specific inducements to encourage the emerging structure described above.

The case of Guyana rum reveals many interesting peculiarities of the industry which are important for industry expansion. Guyana and other Caribbean nations largely export bulk rum into Europe where global lead firms blend, age and bottle. In addition, marketing is critical to upscale product branding, so companies have to be prepared to allocate as much as 19 per cent of sales to this effort in order to win and secure markets. The weight-to-value ratio also brings great value to bottling close to markets. In essence, this implies that the rum business favours those with deep pockets, although it provides tremendous opportunity for deriving surplus value. In the case of Guyana, there are challenges with raw material input that must be resolved for industry expansion based on local molasses input to be successful.

The rum industry might explore collaboration among the key players. In particular, firms and the state should strategize for greater expansion, which could involve the acquisition of an ageing and bottling plant by private producers of bulk rum in the consumer market. To address the shipping challenges, the state must be involved in the provision of a deep-water harbour to accommodate larger ships. Such an investment cannot be justified simply on the needs of the rum industry, so the expanded port facility must be rationalized on the basis of the expansion of other industries that could benefit from it.

The need for human resource training and development stands out as a major inhibitor to growth in several of the cases, particularly Baron, solar power and ship repair. In all instances there was a shortage of training opportunities designed for the specific skilled human resource needs of the industry. Since education in all these countries is largely state driven, a more market needs driven approach to training curriculum development is indicated.

In other instances, as in the case of solar power, it was found that the industry needs to engage in research and development to transcend the current mature stage of the industry. This would require moving to a higher level of value creation to sustain its competitiveness.

Meeting international standards as a prerequisite to competing in export markets emerges as another vital find, requiring investment in standards certification by firms and industry. There is also an important role for national and regional standards institutions – such as the Bureau of Standards in Trinidad and Tobago and its counterpart in other Caribbean countries – to play a greater role in supporting industries in this regard.

Through value chain analysis local firms and industries can gain a strategic understanding of the global markets in which they operate and the strategies which lead firms use to gain and maintain competitive advantage. They can further gain a comprehensive understanding of the value-adding activities which occur along the chain so that decisions with respect to better positioning can be made.

From a policy position, analyses such as these provide market-driven information and state-of-the-industry analyses which can help policymakers to develop targeted initiatives that can support the growth and development of sectors targeted for expansion. In the current circumstances where countries of the Caribbean region are grappling with negative growth and the need for economic diversification, understanding the value chain within which existing industries operate can allow for the efficient alignment of policy to the specific needs of growth strategies which can be distilled from global industry study. In conclusion, what emerges are specific areas which respective firms, industries and policymakers must address in order to capitalize on opportunities for improved competiveness along the value chain continuum and which contributes to the overall growth and sustainable competitiveness of firms, industries and countries.

Note

1. OECD (2013) notes that "the income from trade flows within GVCs has doubled between 1995 and 2009: for China it has increased 6-fold, India 5-fold and Brazil 3-fold".

References

Gereffi, G. 1995. "Global Production Systems and Third World Development". In *Global Change, Regional Response: The New International Context of Development*, edited by B. Stallings, 100–42. New York: Cambridge University Press.
Gereffi, G., and K. Fernandez-Stark. 2011. *Global Value Chain Analysis: A Primer*. Durham, NC: Duke University Center on Globalization, Governance and Competitiveness. http://www.cggc.duke.edu/pdfs/2011-05-31_GVC_analysis_a_primer.pdf.

OECD (Organisation for Economic Co-operation and Development). 2013. *Aid for Trade at a Glance 2013: Connecting to Value Chains.* http://dx.doi.org/10.1787/aid_glance-2013-en.

UNCTAD (United Nations Conference on Trade and Development). 2013. *World Investment Report 2013: Global Value Chains: Investment and Trade for Development.* unctad.org/es/PublicationsLibrary/wir2013_en.pdf.

SECTION 1
Manufacturing Industry Case Studies

CASE STUDY 1

A St Lucian Experience for Sustainable Participation in the Agro-Foods Global Value Chain
The Case of Baron Foods Limited

VIMLAWATTI ST HILL
Certified Management Consultant

JACINTHA LEE
Independent Research Professional

Abstract

The focus of this case study is to provide a blueprint for agro-processing businesses in St Lucia that are interested in exporting their products. The study employed the global value chain (GVC) framework to inform its analysis. The authors used literature reviews and interviews with major stakeholders to determine the strengths and shortcomings of the industry. The research showed that business support services, government policies and strategies, legislative and regulatory frameworks, enabling environments, well-trained workforces, and a defined standards and certification programme are all important for promoting success in the export market.

1.1 Introduction

This case study focuses on providing a blueprint to guide and support agro-processing businesses in St Lucia that are interested in exporting their products. It examines the experience of Baron Foods (St Lucia) Limited (BFL), a locally based firm, as it expanded from being a family-owned entity in the early 1990s to a key regional exporter to the high-value European market. BFL commenced its agro-processing operations in St Lucia in 1991 as a family-owned enterprise specializing in the production of sauces, spices, condiments, essences, dressings and drink cocktails. At first, BFL focused on the domestic market, offering twelve different products and employing twenty-five staff members. However, the company began exporting its products within just two months of operations. By 2013, BFL's staff had tripled, its product line had increased to 160 distinct offerings, and exports to the English- and French-speaking Caribbean, Canada, Germany, Slovakia, United Kingdom and the United States accounted for 55 per cent of the company's sales. At the time of publication, BFL was in the process of expanding its production facilities regionally and had already opened a "satellite plant" in Grenada. There were also plans to expand to Trinidad, providing the firm with a gateway into the South and Central American markets.

In order to identify key lessons for other firms wishing to export and for policymakers hoping to improve the local institutional conditions to support foreign trade, this case seeks to answer the following questions:

- What opportunities were available for BFL to ensure increased production and expansion of its export market?
- What strategies were utilized by BFL to ensure increased production and expansion of its export market?
- What are the local conditions under which BFL operates?
- What action can be taken to maximize opportunities for other firms in the future and address local challenges they may face?

The research for this case study involved interviews, site visits and analysis of data from secondary and tertiary sources. The team interviewed the managing director of BFL on 29 May 2013 and again on 18 June 2013 and conducted interviews with the company's quality control manager on 18 June 2013. Additional primary data was obtained through interviews with personnel from a number of locally based organizations (see appendix 1.1). Data from secondary and tertiary sources was obtained from GVC literature and local, regional and international publications.

The case is structured as follows: To provide context for the firm-level analysis, an overview of the global market in which BFL operates is first presented. After assessing the local industry, we examine BFL's participation within St Lucia and globally, including the Caribbean market, while also highlighting the factors that contributed to the company's success. The study then analyses key factors of the local institutional framework in St Lucia that can enhance or inhibit a firm's potential to expand and export. In closing, key lessons learned from BFL's experience are highlighted and policy recommendations for improving local conditions offered.

1.2 The Global Condiment, Sauces, Dressings and Seasonings Market

The global market for condiments, sauces, dressings and seasonings is growing steadily, with sales forecasted to reach approximately US$77.8 billion by the year 2017 (PRWeb 2012). Although the Caribbean region is not a major exporter of condiments and sauces, comparative data indicates that the global percentage share of exports from St Lucia has increased every year from 2006 to 2010, with the exception of 2009. Globally, the leading exporters are the United States, Mexico, the Dominican Republic and Jamaica. Table 1.1 provides export data for condiments and sauces from St Lucia and the leading countries from 2006 to 2010. For each country, the total value of exports (in US$ millions) is displayed in the left column while its share of global exports is on the right.

1.2.1 The Local Condiment, Sauces, Dressings and Seasonings Market

As one of the leading firms in the region, BFL accounts for a significant share of St Lucia's exports. Table 1.2 shows BFL's local and export sales for all of its products, including condiments, sauces, dressings and seasonings.[1]

Competition is limited in St Lucia. Only two key firms were identified as competitors in the agro-processing industry – Frootsy Foods and Viking Traders. Frootsy Foods was established in 1997 and has twelve employees. The company manufactures fruit jams, juices and jellies, cheeses, condiments, coconut oil, essences, snacks, and household products, such as dishwashing liquid and disinfectant. Fruits and vegetables account for 40 per cent of inputs and are

Table 1.1. Comparative Export Data: Condiments and Sauces (US$ millions)

Year	Total Global Exports	St Lucia $	%	United States $	%	Mexico $	%	Dominican Republic $	%	Jamaica $	%
2006	$5,823	0.480	0.0087	820	13	130	2.3	16	0.28	10.0	0.91
2007	$6,782	0.520	0.0080	950	12	150	1.9	17	0.26	9.1	0.14
2008	$8,235	0.700	0.0089	960	12	150	1.5	23	0.29	11.0	0.14
2009	$8,113	0.490	0.0064	960	12	150	2.0	28	0.37	11.0	0.14
2010	$8,102	0.580	0.0070	1,100	13	180	2.0	32	0.38	13.0	0.16

Source: Observatory of Economic Complexity Database, http://atlas.media.mit.edu.

sourced locally. Nuts, dried fruits, glass bottles, jars and lids, labels, surfactants, colours, fragrances and flavours are imported.

Founded in 1979, Viking Traders is the oldest and largest of the three firms studied. It is family owned and operated. The company manufactures over one hundred products, including condiments, spices, ketchup, liqueur, coffee and rum cake. All raw materials are sourced from St Lucia.[2]

Table 1.3 provides data on these two competitors, focusing on size, certification, levels of export and system efficiency.

Table 1.2. Baron Foods' Local Sales and Exports, 2000–2012

Year	Local US$m	Export US$m	Number of Products	Certifications Achieved
2012	$4.44	$3.70	N/a	FSSC 22000:2010 and HACCP and ISO 22000:2005
2011	$2.60	$2.60	175	
2010	$2.36	$2.15	163	
2009	$2.11	$1.84	163	HACCP and ISO 22000:2005
2008	$2.18	$2.18	148	
2007	$1.85	$1.51	148	
2006	$1.65	$1.50	148	
2005	$1.50	$1.33	148	HACCP
2004	$1.35	$1.11	140	
2003	$1.21	$1.21	140	
2002	$1.10	$0.96	140	

Source: Baron Foods (St Lucia) Ltd.

Table 1.3. Competition in the St Lucia Condiment and Sauces Market

Company	Size (Employees)	Certification	Level of Exports	Export Market	System Efficiency
Frootsy	12	None*	Minimal	Caribbean islands	Local delivery time: 1–2 days Export time: 1 month
Viking Traders	50	HACCP	No data available	Europe, Canada and the Caribbean	No data available

* Frootsy has not pursued certification, noting that the cost associated with certification and standardization is prohibitive, since the attainment of such standards would require a total revamping/renovation/modification of the current infrastructure.

1.3 Baron Foods' Participation in the Condiments and Sauces Global Value Chain

BFL has focused on developing expertise in most major stages of the condiments and sauces value chain, producing final, branded products for its end markets (Europe, the United Kingdom and the Caribbean) and undertaking marketing initiatives to increase sales.[3] They have placed an emphasis on building expertise on consumer tastes in end markets and on understanding the legal and logistical challenges associated with shipping products to these markets. BFL also prioritizes the identification of niche markets. The company relies primarily on an outgrower programme (contract farming) for its raw materials, and is not directly involved in this aspect of production. BFL has focused on maintaining good relationships with its farmers and other input suppliers. Figure 1.1 illustrates the company's participation in the condiments and sauces GVC.

Figure 1.1 breaks down the groups of actors participating in the condiments and sauces value chain. Over time, BFL has leveraged key opportunities to add value to its products. GVC literature refers to this process as "upgrading", and BFL has demonstrated the following three different types of upgrading:

1. *Process upgrading.* The increasing of the efficiency of production, by focusing on standards and certification. BFL has obtained numerous key certifications.
2. *Product upgrading.* The innovation, diversification or improvement of the final product, by regularly improving the line of products. In BFL's case, the labels of the products are changed every five years and new products are introduced on a regular basis.
3. *Functional upgrading.* Increasing the value added by changing the mix of activities conducted within the company (Gereffi, Fernandez-Stark and Psilos 2011). BFL is actively involved in bottling, marketing and branding its products.

1.4 Key Elements Driving Baron Foods' Export Success

Three important factors led to BFL's upgrading success. The company has actively pursued certification and focused on producing high-quality products that meet its consumers' tastes. BFL has ensured that its workforce is sufficiently trained, in order to maintain the company's quality standards. Finally, BFL is an attractive place to work, and this helps to ensure that it has a good supply of workers.

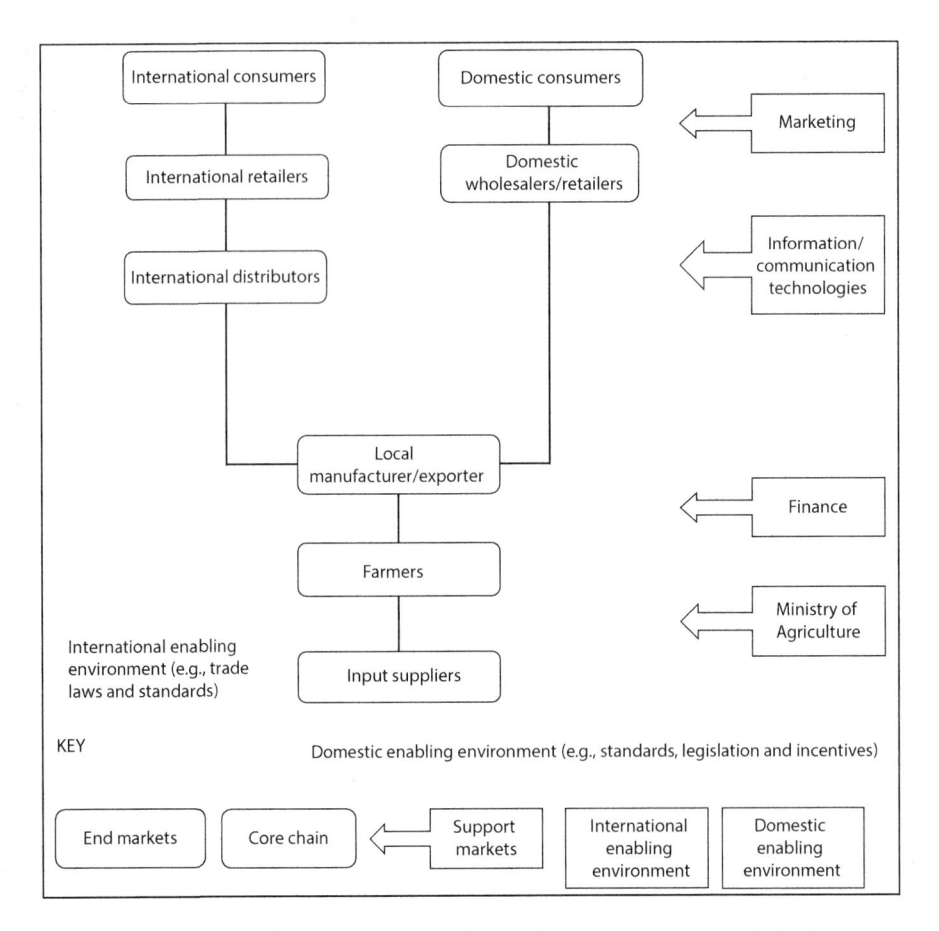

Figure 1.1. Baron Foods' participation in the condiments and sauces global value chain
Source: Authors, adapted from Hesse 2010.

1.4.1 Pursuit of Standards Compliance and Certification

Standards are critical if companies are to gain entry into and sustain competitive advantage within high-value international markets. "Only [companies] that are able to comply with high standards are rewarded with easy access to [these] developed countries markets" (Fernandez-Stark, Bamber and Gereffi 2011).

BFL has invested considerable resources to attain the highest standards possible. The company is committed to ensuring that its products, services and systems conform to quality, safety and performance standards. Some of these standards are voluntary, such as CODEX STAN 160-1987, which is the Codex Standard for mango chutney, and DJS CRS 35:2002, which is the specification for spices and sauces. Other certifications are mandatory if a company wishes to export. In 2003, the company received the Hazard Analysis and Critical Control Points certification before earning the ISO 22000:2005 standard in 2008 and the FSSC 22000:2010 standard in 2011. The FSSC 22000:2010 had important implications in securing market access – only global food giants such as Nestle and Heinz have previously attained this certification.[4]

Meeting these standards has affected BFL's procurement, production, marketing and sales. The company enjoyed increased revenues with a higher volume of sales, and improved efficiency resulted in higher production and improved productivity of the workforce, and better products and sales. The year 2011 recorded an increase of 21 per cent in export sales compared to 2010.

1.4.2 The Role of Training

Workforce development has been identified as one of the key elements of competitiveness participation in GVCs and within GVC upgrading (Gereffi, Fernandez-Stark and Psilos 2011; Cattaneo et al. 2013). In the agro-processing sectors, it has been noted that "specific training (for farmers) is often required to improve productivity and product quality, introduce new technologies and plant varieties, and comply with food safety and other certification requirements that govern entry into the national, regional and international value chains" (Fernandez-Stark, Bamber and Gereffi 2012).

According to the chief executive officer of BFL, Ronald Ramjattan in a 2013 interview, the lack of workforce development in St Lucia is one of the factors impeding the effective growth of the agricultural sector. He attributes this to several issues, including

- Weak linkages with the Ministry of Agriculture, whereby farmers are not visited and as a result do not receive the necessary training.
- Agricultural education is not geared to attract the youth.
- Agricultural methods are not modernized and do not reflect the best training strategies. For example, new propagation methods developed through research conducted by the Ministry of Agriculture are not adequately shared with local farmers. The transfer of this technology is critical to the development of persons involved in the agricultural sector – the lack of which affects crop quality and yield.

The internal strengthening of skills is seen as an important factor in the growth of the company. To overcome these national-level challenges, ensure compliance with standards at all levels and secure quality supply for their processing operations, BFL works closely with five major dedicated farmers, utilizing the outgrower scheme model (Fernandez-Stark, Bamber and Gereffi 2012) whereby farmers are contracted to produce exclusively for the company. These farmers are visited and trained on their farms quarterly. The educational sessions include on-site monitoring by the BFL production or quality control manager; training in areas such as pesticide and fertilizer applications; proper planting of crops; and the utilization of modern methods of farming along with the proper handling and transportation of the crops to the processing facility. Such training is geared towards ensuring adherence to compliance and quality standards. In addition to training, producers receive a number of other benefits, including guarantees that the entire harvest will be purchased, the provision of loans to purchase materials and equipment, and access to water tanks to ensure adequate water supply during the dry season.

In addition to training at the production level, all personnel within the processing facility participate in professional development sessions on a monthly basis, conducted by the quality control manager. Training is also key at the managerial level, particularly with respect to understanding key end markets. These sessions are viewed positively by all levels of employees. As part of BFL's comprehensive quality programme and to ensure export readiness, the company encourages its staff to be creative and develop their skills through the provision of appropriate training. According to a company document, "[i]t is no longer simply a matter of creating a heterogeneous workforce, but using that workforce to create products, services, and business practices that sets Baron Foods apart and gives us that competitive advantage in the export marketplace" (BFL 2013).

1.4.3 The Role of Human Resource Management

To ensure the company's ongoing ability to meet standards and to capture the return on its considerable workforce investment, BFL initiated numerous initiatives to facilitate staff retention. Since the company believes workers who reside in smaller communities display a more positive attitude towards work, it concentrated on recruiting staff from the outskirts of the main town where it is located (Ramjattan interview, 2013). By 2013, the company employed seventy-five persons, three-quarters of whom were female, the majority being drawn from the surrounding communities. Given that applicants with academic qualifications at the graduate level presented problems of effective integration into the company's culture, BFL began to favour hiring "trainable" individuals at the managerial level rather than those who possessed academic qualifications only.

In terms of retention strategies, BFL adopted new measures, including a travel allowance covering 100 per cent of transportation cost; loans for the purchase of children's school supplies (employees are eligible after one year of service); housing loans to employees with over five years of service;[5] assistance with child care; provision of on-site meals that the company subsidizes at 60 per cent (breakfast, lunch and sometimes dinner);[6] and the offering of the use of recreational/sporting facilities.[7] In addition, BFL hosts regular subsidized social events as part of its strategy to understand the frustrations and problems experienced by staff.

These incentives have probably played a role in ensuring that 70 per cent of employees have worked for the company for over fifteen years (40 per cent of employees have been with the company for over twenty years).[8] While the overall attrition rate is low, it is higher among lower-skilled employees who resign mainly because of maternity leave, better job offers and the inability to deal with the challenges associated with certification.

1.4.4 SWOT Analysis of Baron Foods

Table 1.4 provides an overview of the key strengths and weaknesses of BFL and the opportunities and threats it faced when trying to increase its exports.

1.5 Local Industry Conditions: Challenges for Other Firms

Replicating BFL's success requires overcoming significant challenges within the local institutional setting in St Lucia. The sector is highly fragmented and is still small. In addition, there has been no concerted approach to marketing and product development to date. Despite the fact that the sector was identified by the Ministry of Agriculture as a key driver for employment creation in rural areas, no comprehensive sector-wide approach to facilitating growth has been developed (St Lucia Ministry of Agriculture 2013). Table 1.5 outlines the local industry conditions through an analysis of the following factors: productive capacity, infrastructure and services, business environment, trade and investment policy, and institutionalization. These factors have been identified as being

Table 1.4. SWOT Analysis of Baron Foods

Strengths	Weaknesses
• Ability to meet high quality requirements of the international market and strong export orientation • Established connections to the target markets (local, regional and global) with the experience to expand reach • Diverse product range with strong brand presence and established niche markets • Qualified and experienced personnel • Strategic alliances • Adequate financial resources for funding • Openness to engage in public-private partnerships	• High cost of inputs • Limited availability of appropriate skills • Inconsistency of quality and supply of raw materials • Weak coordination among policy and service entities (government ministries and corporations) • Difficulty in obtaining data and other market intelligence
Opportunities	**Threats**
• Continue to expand regionally and internationally based on strong demand for the Baron brand • Continue to diversify product range based on knowledge of consumers	• Poor local and global economic climate • Political instability • Growing competition, both regionally and internationally • Continued increase in labour costs without corresponding productivity improvements • Poor perception of agriculture as a viable economic sector, which will lead to reduction in the number of farmers • Lack of clear agricultural and investment policies • Outdated fiscal incentive policy • Weather conditions impact on regular supply of raw material

instrumental in supporting the upgrading of firms and countries in regional and global value chains.

As seen in table 1.5, there are several factors affecting the island's level of competitiveness in the agro-processing GVC. A critical factor is productive capacity,

Table 1.5. Factors Affecting St Lucia's Competitiveness in the Agro-Processing Global Value Chain

Factor		Description
Productive capacity	Human capital	There is training of workers at all levels of the process. Since certification requires record-keeping, a number of workers are challenged because of deficiencies in literacy and numeracy. They are unable to cope with the rigors necessary for certification.
	Standards and certification	Of the three players in the sector, one (Frootsy) has not attained any certification, two (Viking Traders and BFL) have attained HACCP certification and only one (BFL) has achieved ISO 22000:2005 and FSSC 22000:2010 standards. The audit for such certification standards for BFL was undertaken by SGS – an accreditation body headquartered in Geneva, Switzerland.
	National system of innovation	
Infrastructure and services	Transportation, ICT, energy and water	The cost of energy and water continues to increase. Transportation from the Caribbean also continues to be a key cost for exports to Europe and Asia.
Business environment	Macroeconomic stability and public governance	The Eastern Caribbean currency is pegged against the US dollar and the rate is fixed. Although the rates against other currencies fluctuate on a daily basis, this does not seem to have an adverse effect on the island's ability to generate revenue from its exports.
	Ease of opening a business and permitting/ licensing	The island is ranked 53 of 185 countries in the World Bank 2013 report on the ease of doing business. • Starting a business: Ranked 51st • Dealing with construction permits: Ranked 11th • Getting electricity: Ranked 12th
	Access to finance	Access to finance/getting credit is much weaker, coming at 104th in the same report.

(Table 1.5 continues)

Table 1.5. Factors Affecting St Lucia's Competitiveness in the Agro-Processing Global Value Chain (*continued*)

Factor		Description
Trade and investment policy	Market access	(To all markets)
	Import tariffs	Tariffs charged on imported components
	Export-import procedures	Customs documents needed to export – 5; Cost of export of one container up to the local seaport amounts to US$1,375. Customs documents needed to import – 9
	Border transit times	Time to export – 14 days; Time to import – 17 days
	Industry-specific policies	Policies not currently in place
Institutionalization	Industry maturity and coordination	Farmers possess a high level of experience and are well represented on various farmers' associations. As a result they benefit from reduced costs for input supplies and other incentives. Business partnerships among different players in the marketplace are weak. Linkages with international organizations – weak
	Public-private coordination	Linkages with the Ministry of Agriculture – weak; Linkages with the Ministry of Commerce – good; Attitude of public officials – hindrance to trade

Source: Author's compilation based on Bamber and Fernandez-Stark 2013.

which encompasses the training of workers and the pursuit of certifications. The training of workers at all levels of the process is essential, since the acquisition of certification requires workers to possess the necessary skills for dealing with the level of documentation required. With respect to the acquisition of globally recognized certification, only BFL has achieved ISO 22000:2005 and FSSC 22000:2010 standards. This can be attributed to BFL's comprehensive training efforts, from farmers to the managerial level.

Another critical factor is institutionalization, which refers to industry maturity and coordination along with public-private coordination. Business partnerships among different players in the market in St Lucia are weak. This deficiency also extends to linkages with international organizations. However, the involvement of farmers in the BFL process has been cited as having a positive effect since they are very experienced and involved in various farmers' associations. Involvement in such groupings provides an opportunity for farmers to benefit from various incentives, including a reduction in the cost of supplies.

1.6 Lessons Learned

Key lessons can be drawn from the analysis of BFL's success as an exporter in the agro-processing GVC. These lessons can be leveraged by other companies seeking to enter competitive export markets. These main lessons are highlighted in table 1.6.

1.7 Policy Recommendations for Sector Development

The recommendations outlined below focus on the following key areas: (1) the provision of appropriate incentives; (2) regulations to improve efficiency; (3) effective coordination of the industry; and (4) the provision of relevant education and training activities.

1.7.1 Provision of Appropriate Incentives

- An incentive programme should be implemented by the St Lucia Bureau of Standards for prospective exporters who hope to introduce standards to become export ready.
- Modern farming techniques, such as the use of greenhouses, should be promoted among all farmers and incentives should be given to farmers to use modern technology.

1.7.2 Regulations to Improve Efficiency

- Exporters should be placed on a priority list to allow for greater efficiency and quick turnaround time for processing documentation.

Table 1.6. Lessons Learned from Baron Foods' Evolution as an Exporter

Lessons Learned	Factors
1. Approach business in a creative and collaborative fashion	Bring together collective views from all staff members
2. Invest in a well-trained workforce	The company boasts a diverse and inclusive workforce that allows for creativity, new ideas and innovation
3. Innovation and product upgrading is important in order to keep abreast of changes in customer tastes and preferences	Innovation created the competitive advantage that led to company growth
4. Implementation of new processes for standards compliance and certification is critical to the success in a value chain	Management's insistence on obtaining certification contributed to the entrance of products into the local and international markets
5. Identification of niche markets is a critical factor	BFL conducted the necessary research on the niche markets and then made the appropriate changes for entry into these markets
6. Take advantage of all the incentives and concessions provided by government	The company utilized the incentives that reduced the cost of production, allowing BFL to be more competitive in the export market
7. High level of foresight and vision from management	This outlook has allowed for the continued sustainability of BFL
8. Avoid the introduction of a wide range of products within a short space of time	New products were introduced within a short period, creating a problem in the marketplace, especially with regard to shelf space in supermarkets

- Policymakers play a critical role in the creation of an enabling environment; therefore, the legal and regulatory framework must be improved so as to encourage both exporters and farmers.
- The legal and regulatory framework must be upgraded to take into account the needs of exporters and farmers. Therefore, it is recommended that discussions regarding required improvements should include a wide range of actors from the business sector.

1.7.3 Effective Coordination of the Industry

- For upgrading and value chain development to be successful, linkages must be strengthened among the relevant stakeholders. This will facilitate the sharing of information and create greater cohesiveness and efficiency.
- Bring together stakeholders who possess knowledge, skills and resources to develop and deliver appropriate financial products and services.

1.7.4 Provision of Relevant Education and Training Activities

- An innovative and productive sector requires more highly skilled workers with a mix of skills. This should be addressed by an education and training policy geared towards the export sector. In order to build capacity, greater emphasis should be placed on educational institutions such as the Sir Arthur Community College and University of the West Indies (Open Campus).
- Introduce agriculture in all schools starting from the primary level, thereby allowing youth to have a better understanding of agriculture as a potential career option.
- There should be regular visits by extension officers to farmers. These officers can provide valuable advice and guidance.

In conclusion, the management of BFL understood the importance of operating within the local, regional and global agro-processing value chains, identifying niche product opportunities in key markets and ensuring strong coordination throughout the supply chain in order to maintain export competitiveness.

Notes

1. Appendix 1.4 provides data on the total export of specific condiments.
2. Efforts to obtain primary data from Viking Traders were unsuccessful, so information had to be sourced from the company's website.
3. The company uses a multitalented team with the focus on quality assurance, merchandising and export. There is no marketing department or sales manager – marketing is coordinated within the office of the chief executive officer. Research is conducted on a regular basis to determine new markets.

4. Other standards and regulations adopted by BFL are outlined in appendix 1.3.
5. Loans range from US$1,840 to US$36,806.
6. Credit is also extended to provide for the purchase of meals.
7. The company built a gym specifically for staff and subsidized 60 per cent of membership fees.
8. Similar employment strategies have been used in more developed countries to recruit and retain labour (Fernandez-Stark, Bamber and Gereffi 2011).

References

Bamber, P., and Fernandez-Stark, K. 2013. "Global Value Chains, Economic Upgrading and Gender in the Horticulture Industry". In *Global Value Chains, Economic Upgrading, and Gender: Case Studies of the Horticulture, Tourism and Call Center Industries*, edited by C. Staritz. Washindon, DC: World Bank. http://www.cggc.duke.edu/pdfs/GVC_Gender_Report_web_2013.pdf.

BFL (Baron Foods [St Lucia] Ltd). 2013. "Success in Export: Baron Foods". Presentation at the Caribbean Exporters Colloquium, Barbados, 20–21 March.

Cattaneo, O., G. Gereffi, S. Miroudot and D. Taglioni. 2013. *Joining Upgrading and Being Competitive in Global Value Chains: A Strategic Framework*. Washington, DC: World Bank. http://www.cggc.duke.edu/pdfs/2013-404_WorldBank_wps6406_Cattaneo_Gereffi_Miroudot_Taglioni_Competitiveness_GVCs.pdf.

Fernandez-Stark, K., P. Bamber and G. Gereffi. 2011. *The Fruit and Vegetables Global Value Chain: Economic Upgrading and Workforce Development*. Durham, NC: Duke University Center on Globalization, Governance and Competitiveness. http://www.cggc.duke.edu/pdfs/2011-11-10_CGGC_Fruit-and-Vegetables-Global-Value-Chain.pdf.

———. 2012. *Inclusion of Small- and Medium-Sized Producers in High-Value Global Agro Food Value Chains*. Durham, NC: Duke University Center on Globalization, Governance and Competitiveness. http://www.cggc.duke.edu/pdfs/2012-05_Duke CGGC_InclusiveBusiness_and_HighValueAgricultureValueChains_v2.pdf.

Gereffi, G., K. Fernandez-Stark and P. Psilos. 2011. *Skills for Upgrading: Workforce Development and Global Value Chains in Developing Countries*. Durham, NC: Duke University Center on Globalization, Governance and Competitiveness.

James, J., T. Haynes, V. Fontenelle, X. Dubuison, J. King and D. Gerundino. 2013. "Economic Benefits of Standards (Pilot Study) Baron Foods (St Lucia) Ltd".

PRWeb. 2012. "Global Condiments, Sauces, Dressings, and Seasonings Market to Reach US$77.8 Billion by 2017". 3 April. http://www.prweb.com/releases/Condiments/Seasonings/prweb9364006.htm.

St Lucia. Ministry of Agriculture. 2013. "Action Fiche for St Lucia, ACP/Caribbean Agriculture".

Appendix 1.1 Sources of Primary Data

Individual team members conducted interviews with personnel from the following agencies/organizations:

- Ministry of Agriculture
- St Lucia Air and Sea Ports Authority
- Frosty Foods
- Inter-American Institute for Cooperation on Agriculture
- St Lucia Trade Export Promotion Agency
- St Lucia Bureau of Standards
- Ministry of Commerce
- St Lucia Chamber of Commerce
- St Lucia Manufacturers' Association
- Government of St Lucia Statistics Department.

The team conducted site visits to the BFL processing facility located in the south of the island and to one of the farms supplying inputs to the company.

Appendix 1.2 Baron Foods' Organizational Chart

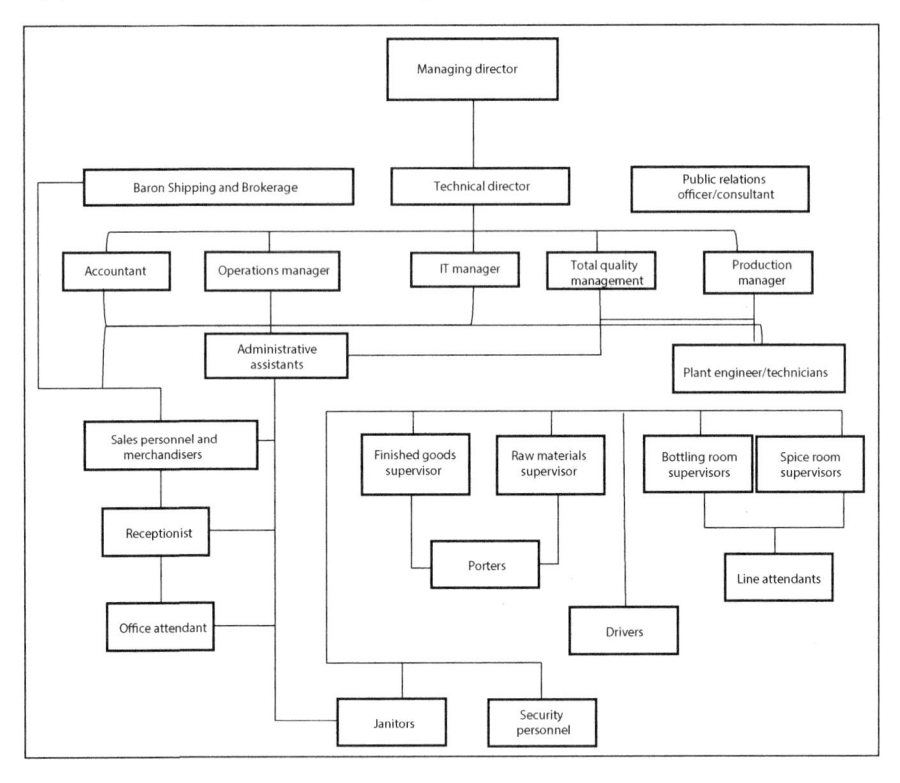

```
                          ┌───────────────────┐
                          │ Managing director │
                          └─────────┬─────────┘
                                    │
        ┌───────────────────────────┼───────────────────────────┐
        │                           │                           │
┌───────┴──────────────┐  ┌─────────┴─────────┐  ┌──────────────┴──────┐
│ Baron Shipping and   │  │ Technical director│  │ Public relations    │
│ Brokerage            │  │                   │  │ officer/consultant  │
└──────────────────────┘  └─────────┬─────────┘  └─────────────────────┘
                                    │
    ┌──────────┬────────────────────┼────────────────────┬──────────────┐
┌───┴──────┐ ┌─┴────────────┐ ┌─────┴─────┐ ┌────────────┴────┐ ┌───────┴────┐
│Accountant│ │Operations    │ │IT manager │ │Total quality    │ │Production  │
│          │ │manager       │ │           │ │management       │ │manager     │
└──────────┘ └──────┬───────┘ └───────────┘ └─────────────────┘ └─────┬──────┘
                    │                                                  │
             ┌──────┴─────────┐                              ┌─────────┴──────────┐
             │ Administrative │                              │ Plant engineer/    │
             │ assistants     │                              │ technicians        │
             └────────────────┘                              └────────────────────┘

┌──────────────┐  ┌───────────┐ ┌───────────┐ ┌───────────┐ ┌───────────┐
│Sales personnel│  │Finished   │ │Raw        │ │Bottling   │ │Spice room │
│and merchandisers│ │goods     │ │materials  │ │room       │ │supervisors│
│              │  │supervisor │ │supervisor │ │supervisors│ │           │
└──────┬───────┘  └─────┬─────┘ └─────┬─────┘ └───────────┘ └─────┬─────┘
       │                └──────┬──────┘                           │
┌──────┴───────┐              ┌┴────────┐                  ┌──────┴──────┐
│ Receptionist │              │ Porters │                  │Line attendants│
└──────┬───────┘              └─────────┘                  └─────────────┘
       │
┌──────┴───────┐                       ┌─────────┐
│Office attendant│                     │ Drivers │
└──────────────┘                       └─────────┘

                    ┌─────────┐   ┌──────────┐
                    │ Janitors│   │ Security │
                    │         │   │ personnel│
                    └─────────┘   └──────────┘
```

Source: Baron Foods (St Lucia) Ltd 2013.

Appendix 1.3 Standards and Regulations Used by Baron Foods

Required
HACCP
ISO 22000:2005 Food Safety Management Systems
FSSC 22000:2010 Food Safety System Certification
PAS 220:2008 Food Safety Requirements for Food Manufacturing
Canada regulations for processed food
Contaminants in food in the United Kingdom
European Union regulations
Regulations Amending the Food and Drug Regulations (1200 – Enhanced labelling for food allergen and gluten sources and added sulphites): PC 2011-80; 3 February 2011
Commission Regulation (EC) No 1881/2006 of 19 December 2006: setting maximum levels of certain contaminants in foodstuffs

Voluntary
CODEX STAN 160-1987: Codex standard for mango chutney
DJS CRS 35:2002 Specification for spices and sauces

Source: James et al. 2013.

Appendix 1.4 Total Export of Condiments – St Lucia

Ranking on Commodity	FOB Value (EC$) 2008	Net Weight (Kg) 2008	FOB Value (EC$) 2009	Net Weight (Kg) 2009	FOB Value (EC$) 2010	Net Weight (Kg) 2010	FOB Value (EC$) 2011	Net Weight (Kg) 2011
21032010 – Tomato ketchup	*24,132*	*18,442*	*12,386*	*9,445*	*290,134*	*150,788*	*258,412*	*187,544*
Anguilla	–	–	169	48	–	–	–	–
Barbados	–	–	–	–	148	27	–	–
Bonaire/Saba/St Eustatius	–	–	300	4	–	–	–	–
Guyana	20,913	18,082	10,901	9,163	1,289	9,527	13,696	10,758
United Kingdom	–	–	–	–	1,038	106	–	–
United States	–	–	1,016	210	–	–	91	15
US Virgin Islands	3,219	360	–	–	–	–	–	–
St Lucia	–	–	–	–	190,764	99,808	–	–
Country of Production	–	–	–	–	85,287	41,320	244,626	176,770
21039010 – Pepper sauce	*1,117,449*	*190,597*	*1,028,151*	*164,107*	*1,124,223*	*225,584*	*1,159,377*	*310,406*
Anguilla	430	44	–	–	–	–	–	–
Antigua and Barbuda	–	–	–	–	1,949	261	–	–
Bonaire/Saba/St Eustatius	–	–	6,080	10	–	–	–	–
Barbados	23,151	4,091	31,604	5,495	29,189	5,410	29,766	7,038
Canada	835	75	170	55	163	0	–	–
Spain	4	3	–	–	–	–	–	–
United Kingdom	173,681	24,962	129,414	21,258	146,948	21,756	96,749	21,148

Grenada	226,187	35,514	253,636	40,014	5,434	1,224	–	–
Guyana	39,486	32,958	19,701	16,229	21,377	16,640	35,088	29,080
Haiti	12,370	2,999	–	–	12,702	2,999	–	–
Jamaica	49,964	7,408	51,021	6,609	–	–	–	–
St Kitts/Nevis	9,509	1,455	–	–	–	–	–	–
St Lucia	–	–	–	–	134,948	62,187	–	–
Martinique	68,533	7,274	84,010	10,032	114,870	12,350	87,369	10,652
Netherlands	–	–	–	–	2,619	328	–	–
Puerto Rico	43,281	4,518	26,436	2,689	26,098	2,615	57,561	7,237
St Maarten	54,485	6,062	45,254	4,740	36,639	3,522	69,561	10,936
Trinidad and Tobago	–	–	–	–	139	15	203	20
United States	274,323	44,052	278,301	46,679	420,756	57,946	408,247	79,291
British Virgin Islands	5,090	494	2,488	247	3,122	276	789	143
USVirgin Islands	136,120	18,688	100,036	10,050	106,162	10,827	148,607	26,147
Country of Production	–	–	–	–	61,109	27,023	226,437	118,714
21039020 – Mayonnaise	*4,354*	*2,291*	*2,646*	*1,156*	*14,008*	*4,625*	*30,442*	*8,414*
United Kingdom	–	–	–	–	112	10	–	–
Guyana	4,354	2,291	2,646	1,155	2,457	1,096	1,999	284
St Lucia	–	–	–	–	5,007	1,602	–	–
Country of Production	–	–	–	–	6,432	1,917	29,243	8,130

Source: Government of St Lucia Statistical Department.

CASE STUDY 2

A Structural Analysis of the Competitiveness of the Hot Pepper Sauce Industry in Trinidad and Tobago
A Global Value Chain Approach

SHELLYANNE WILSON
Lecturer in Operations Management
Department of Management Studies
University of the West Indies, St Augustine

Abstract

This case study presents an analysis of the Trinidad and Tobago hot pepper sauce industry, using the global value chain (GVC) methodology to identify opportunities to increase the industry's participation in value chains. The GVC methodology attempts to identify the activities and actors who contribute inputs and value-adding services towards a final output. The suppliers, processors, and sales and distribution channels of the Trinidad and Tobago hot pepper sauce industry are described, as well as its supporting and relating institutions. The study also uses Porter's (1990) diamond model to examine the competitiveness of the industry, finding that the limited supply of fresh hot peppers and pepper mash was a major inhibitor to productivity.

To increase the local hot pepper industry's participation in GVCs, three upgrading strategies were identified. Under product upgrading, the local hot pepper sauce industry can expand its product lines into the "fiery food" segment by incorporating hot pepper sauce into other sauces and condiments. Under expansion along the chain, the local hot pepper sauce industry can engage in specialized pepper mash manufacturing and private label pepper sauce production via contract manufacturing. Finally, under end market or channel upgrading, the local hot pepper sauce industry can seek entry into non-traditional markets. Policy recommendations to support upgrading are also presented.

2.1 Introduction

The hot pepper sauce industry in Trinidad and Tobago can be traced to the 1960s and is characterized by at least two categories of pepper sauce manufacturers: medium and large food manufacturing companies with multiple products, including hot sauce, and a rapidly growing number of small hot sauce producers that specialize in hot sauce and other types of seasonings.

The flourishing hot pepper sauce industry can be partially credited to Trinidad and Tobago's supply of some of the hottest peppers in the world, which are then used as the primary raw input. There is also a growing market for hot pepper sauce globally. These conditions combine to present multiple opportunities for producers in Trinidad and Tobago to target different segments in the local, regional and global markets. However, while the larger firms have been able to penetrate the traditional international diaspora markets of Miami and New York in the United States, Toronto in Canada, and London in the United Kingdom, they have had less success expanding beyond those major markets. Furthermore, the small and micro firms have had trouble growing to the point where they could be expected to export their products outside Trinidad and Tobago.

This case study will present an analysis of the hot pepper sauce industry by examining the sector in Trinidad and Tobago and the global marketplace to determine how local firms can expand into non-traditional markets. It makes use of the GVC methodology to identify opportunities for improving the competitiveness of the Trinidad and Tobago hot pepper sauce industry. The case study proceeds as follows:

- Section 2.2 presents the GVC for the hot pepper sauce industry.
- Section 2.3 provides an overview of the Trinidad and Tobago hot pepper sauce industry.
- Section 2.4 examines the local conditions and competitiveness factors.
- Section 2.5 outlines a number of upgrading strategies and tactics for the hot pepper industry.
- Section 2.6 outlines key lessons learned from the case study.
- Section 2.7 presents recommendations and conclusions.

2.2 The Hot Pepper Sauce Global Value Chain

The GVC for the hot pepper sauce industry is illustrated in figure 2.1 and shows the activities, actors and products along the value chain. The activities include

	Activities					
Inputs	Chilli pepper production	Chilli paste production	Packing and storage	Hot sauce production	Distribution and marketing	

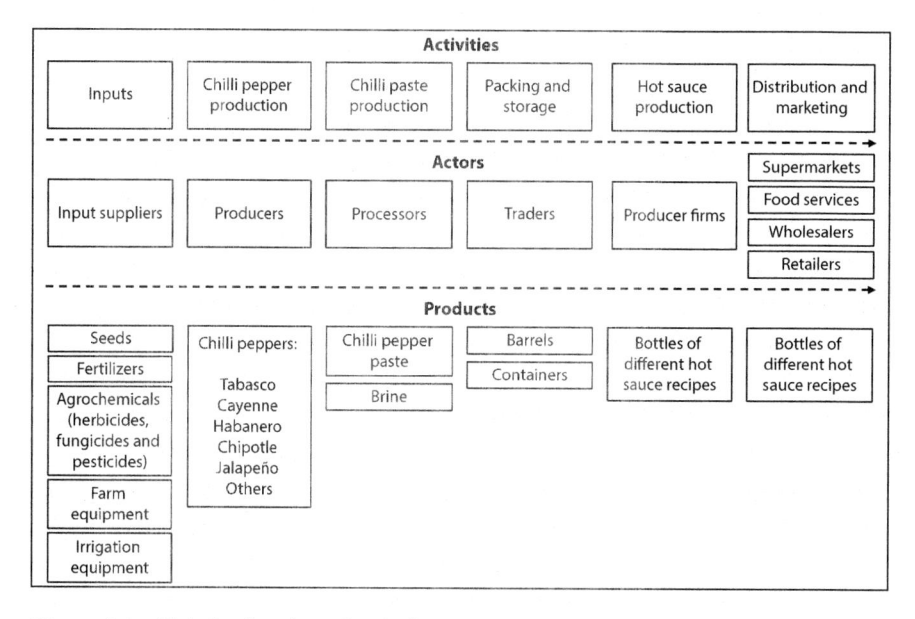

	Actors					
Input suppliers	Producers	Processors	Traders	Producer firms	Supermarkets	
					Food services	
					Wholesalers	
					Retailers	

	Products					
Seeds	Chilli peppers:	Chilli pepper paste	Barrels	Bottles of different hot sauce recipes	Bottles of different hot sauce recipes
Fertilizers	Tabasco		Containers		
Agrochemicals (herbicides, fungicides and pesticides)	Cayenne Habanero Chipotle Jalapeño Others	Brine			
Farm equipment					
Irrigation equipment					

Figure 2.1. Global value chain for the hot pepper sauce industry

chilli pepper production, chilli pepper paste or mash production, packing and storage of hot pepper paste or mash, hot pepper sauce production, and the distribution and marketing of the sauce (Meléndez and Uribe 2012).

While there are actors who specialize in individual areas, there are also fully integrated actors whose activities span the entire chain. Likewise, there are actors who engage in some, but not all, activities.

2.3 Hot Pepper Production

Peppers are generally classified as sweet peppers, bell peppers and hot peppers or chillis.[1] Hot peppers or chillis are distinguished from bell peppers and sweet peppers based on their pungency, which is caused by the compound capsaicin. The pungency, measured in terms of Scoville heat units, range from low values of 5,000 Scoville heat units for jalapenos, to medium values for Scotch bonnet of 250,000–300,000, to high values for Bhut Jolokia of over 1 million (Liu and Nair 2010). In 2012, the Trinidad Moruga Scorpion Pepper was reported to be the world's hottest pepper, with its pungency measuring over 2 million Scoville heat units (Bosland, Coon and Reeves 2012).

There has been growth in terms of global hot pepper production. In 2004, the total world production of fresh green chilli peppers and fresh red chilli peppers was 24 million tonnes and 2.5 million tonnes, respectively. For both types, Asia was the highest production region with China leading fresh green chilli pepper production (12 million tonnes) and India producing the most fresh red chilli peppers with 1.1 million tonnes (Chile Pepper Institute 2005). Mexico, Turkey, Indonesia and the United States are among the other important producers of green peppers.

The concentration of hot pepper–producing countries in Asia, South and Central America, and Africa is attributed both to the favourable climatic conditions that are suitable for the growing of hot peppers and also to low labour costs. The latter is of particular importance since harvesting of hot peppers is done manually (Richardson 2012).

Within the production stage of the value chain, firms operate in a number of ways: some cultivate peppers for stock seed that is then sold to other farmers for use in production, some grow hot peppers to sell in the open market or to specific buyers under contractual arrangements and others grow and use the peppers in downstream processing activities.

2.4 Hot Pepper Paste/Mash Production

Hot pepper paste or mash is made by grinding hot peppers, adding ingredients such as salt and vinegar, and then packaging the paste or mash to allow the mixture to age for a specified period of time. Hot pepper sauce processors sometimes prefer using hot pepper mash over fresh hot peppers for three main reasons – greater intensity of the flavour, the ease of handling, and the ability to age or cure the product for as much as three years (*NOU Magazine* 2000).

The global distribution of pepper mash producers is similar to the chilli pepper production network. In the Western Hemisphere, Mexico, Columbia, Costa Rica and Ecuador are the most prominent producers. Firms sell pepper mash on the open market or to buyers under contract. Additionally, there are pepper mash producers who use the mash in their downstream processing activities.

2.5 Hot Pepper Sauce Production

The companies that concentrate on hot pepper sauce production vary by size and product focus.[2] McIlhenny Company is one example of a specialty hot sauce company. The Tabasco brand of the McIlhenny Company is considered to be the global leader in the hot pepper sauce industry while a number of local and regional producers compete with the Tabasco brand in local and regional markets. No company poses a global challenge (Meléndez and Uribe 2012).

There are large food multinational corporations that produce a full range of food products. They are entering the "fiery foods" segment, where spicy ingredients are incorporated into food items such as snack foods and condiments. For example, Heinz introduced a range of hot sauces in 2012 – chipotle and garlic hot sauce, green jalapeño pepper sauce and habanero pepper sauce. Recently, multinational corporations and specialty hot sauce companies have engaged in cross-brand product partnerships; in 2012, Unilever and the US-based Frank's Red Hot collaborated in the production of Hellmann's Spicy Buffalo Light Mayonnaise.

Finally, there is a large segment of smaller hot sauce producers, particularly in countries where there is a high demand for hot sauces. Firms in this emerging segment of the market are producing hot sauces with different types, flavours and degrees of intensity. Additionally, there are contract based manufacturers who produce different hot pepper sauces for private labels.

Table 2.1 outlines characteristics about the two categories of lead firms in the pepper sauce production stage of the hot pepper sauce GVC (hot pepper sauce producers or larger multinational corporations that produce a variety of condiments).

Table 2.1. Lead Firms by Parent Industry and by Market

Category	Company	Key Brands	Headquarters
Hot sauce industry	Reckitt Benckiser	Frank's Redhot	United States
	McIlhenny Tabasco Sauce	Tabasco	United States
	TW Garner Food Company	Texas Pete Hot Sauce	United States
	Jose Cuervo S.A. de C.V.	Cholula Hot Sauce	Mexico
Condiments and sauces industry	Unilever	Hellmann's, Knorr	United Kingdom, The Netherlands
	HJ Heinz Co.		
	Campbell Soup Co.	Heinz	United States
	Hormel Foods Co.	Campbell	United States
	J.M. Smuckers Co.	Hormel, Skippy	United States
		Smuckers	United States

Source: Tully and Holland 2010.

2.6 Overview of the Hot Pepper Sauce Industry in Trinidad and Tobago

Trinidad and Tobago's food and beverage sector exported US$280 million in 2010 (Citibank 2011) and was responsible for 4.8 per cent of the country's gross domestic product in 2012 (GORTT 2013). The hot pepper industry is a relatively small segment of the overall food and beverage processing sector – its estimated value was US$15.6 million in 2010 (CARDI 2011).

All segments of the value chain are present in the local hot pepper industry: the fresh hot pepper segment, the hot pepper mash segment, the dried hot pepper segment and the hot pepper sauce segment.

While the global hot pepper industry was the focus of the previous section, this portion of the study considers each segment of the chain as they exist in Trinidad and Tobago by providing a brief overview of selected players in the Trinidad and Tobago hot pepper sauce industry. The most prominent actors are processors, suppliers, and sales and distribution providers. Supporting institutions include research and technical support organizations, business support institutions, financial institutions, and government and statutory agencies.

2.7 Actors in Trinidad and Tobago's Value Chain

2.7.1 Suppliers

Suppliers in the value chain include sellers of raw materials, intermediate goods, packaging materials, and processing and packaging equipment. Suppliers of the main raw material – hot peppers – include local farms. The supply of fresh hot pepper production in Trinidad and Tobago has declined in the last decade – after 1,050 tonnes were collected in 2001, production fell to 350 tonnes in 2012 (Ministry of Food Production, Land and Marine Affairs 2012). To meet this shortfall and to satisfy local demand, hot peppers are imported from regional countries and sold via farmers' markets.

Pepper mash is the major intermediate good. It is supplied locally by companies such as the Trinidad and Tobago Agribusiness Association, which has a network of over 200 farmers and the production facilities to produce, store and supply pepper mash to local, regional and international hot pepper sauce producers. To meet the demand of the industry, pepper mash is also imported from manufacturers in countries such as Costa Rica and Columbia. Owing to lower labour, packaging and raw material costs, Costa Rican pepper mash is significantly cheaper than pepper mash from the Trinidad and Tobago Agribusiness Association (Caribbean Export Development Agency 2004).

Packaging material is primarily sourced from local producers. Glass bottles and jars are manufactured by Carib Glassworks and sold by distributors such as Ibrahim's Poultry, Fruit and Pet Supplies, which also provides caps and seals. Plastic bottles and caps are sold by companies such as Ansa Polymer. Labels are sourced from printers such as Ansa Polymer, Label House, iChris Industries and Cariflex, and cartons are sourced from packaging producers such as Caribbean Packaging Industries. Lastly, commercial processing and packaging machines are typically imported and sold by companies such as Label House.

2.7.2 Hot Pepper Sauce Processors

Hot pepper sauce processors can be subdivided by size and main activity into five major groups: large commercial processors, medium commercial processors, small processors, micro-processors, and restaurants that make their own house hot pepper sauce (see table 2.2).

- **Large commercial processors**: The large commercial processors employ more than fifty workers and are typically diversified manufacturers of a range of sauces, condiments and dressings, and other food products. These companies began as small, family-owned businesses in the 1950s and 1960s and have advanced to the point where they now distribute their products locally, regionally and internationally.
- **Medium commercial processors**: The medium commercial processors employ between twenty-five and fifty workers and manufacture pepper sauces and other food products that are sold locally and regionally, with only a few exporting to international customers. Established in the 1980s and 1990s, these companies, like their larger counterparts, evolved from small, family-owned businesses into bigger firms.
- **Small processors**: The small processors employ from six to twenty-five workers and typically focus on the manufacture of pepper sauce and a small range of other sauces that use local herbs and spices. These processors usually market their product as being "handmade" or "all natural" and free from artificial flavourings and preservatives. They often use fruits and vegetables to create specially flavoured pepper

Table 2.2. Characteristics of Hot Pepper Sauce Processors

Characteristics	Large Processors	Medium Processors	Small Processors	Micro-processors	Restaurant Processors
Number of employees)	+50	25–50	6–25	<6	Range of small – large firms
Export destinations	Yes CARICOM United States Canada United Kingdom	Yes CARICOM United States Canada United Kingdom	Small no. export United Kingdom most common destination	None	None
Products	Full product range of condiments, sauces, dressings Additional product lines include essences, juices, dried spices and seasonings, canned fruits and vegetables	Sauces, seasonings, essences	Pepper sauces and other sauces and seasonings	Pepper sauces and other sauces and seasonings	Main business is food preparation and service Manufacture of pepper sauces and other sauces and seasonings is a secondary but differentiating activity to enhance food served

Value chain activities	Processing, bottling, marketing	Processing, bottling, marketing	Processing, bottling, marketing	Processing, bottling, direct sales	Processing, bottling, negligible direct sales
Ownership	Limited liability companies	Limited liability companies	Limited liability companies	Sole proprietorship/ family owned	
	Local ownership Established as a family-owned business that later expanded	Local ownership Typically family owned	Local ownership	Local ownership; often unregistered	
Examples	National Canners Chief Brand	RHS Marketing Ltd Caribbean Spices Chatak/Food Products	Caribbean Specialty Foods	Cratefoods LilliBelle Bertie's Pepper Sauce Hott Source	Royal Castle KamWah Adam's Bagels Buzo OsteriaItaliana

Source: Author's compilation.

sauces and sometimes experiment with other types of ingredients such as rum to flavour the hot pepper sauces. These processors primarily supply the local market, but they also engage in limited exports, and tend to use avenues such as social media and their own websites to attract foreign sales.
- **Micro-processors**: The micro-processors employ less than six workers and operate in a similar manner as the small processors. Beyond the size difference, micro-processors are unique in that some are unregistered businesses and operate informally.
- **Restaurants manufacturing house pepper sauce**: A number of restaurants produce their own specialty hot pepper sauce that is used primarily as an ingredient by the chefs in the establishment's dishes or as a food enhancer for patrons. Some restaurants also bottle and sell their products.

2.7.3 Sales and Distribution Providers

The large commercial processors distribute their products domestically through supermarkets and groceries. Outside Trinidad and Tobago, these large firms utilize in-house departments, export agents and overseas distributors. The medium-sized processors also distribute their products locally in supermarkets and grocers; the minority that export use export agents and distributors. Small and micro-processors typically distribute their products directly to their customers or in small retail outlets, such as minimarts. A number of the small and micro-processors also target tourists by packaging their products as gift items and placing them in gift and souvenir shops. There are also specialty distributing channels that cater to specialty products – artisan fairs (UpMarket) and specialty distributors (Malabar Farms, Peppercorns, BeFree Foods and Gourmet Genie) are among the most prominent. These processors also use the Internet as another means of creating product awareness and selling their sauces.

2.7.4 Supporting and Related Industries and Organizations

The supporting institutions and organizations for the hot pepper sauce industry include research and technical support institutions, business support institutions, financial institutions and government and statutory agencies.

2.7.5 Research and Technical Support Institutions

The research and technical support institutions that provide research, testing and laboratory services to the industry include the Caribbean Agricultural Research and Development Institute, the University of the West Indies, the University of Trinidad and Tobago, and the Caribbean Industrial Research Institute. In terms of the hot pepper industry, the Caribbean Agricultural Research and Development Institute, the University of the West Indies, and the University of Trinidad and Tobago focus on identifying, producing and enhancing indigenous hot pepper varieties, land preparation and planting, crop maintenance and harvesting and post-harvesting techniques. The Caribbean Industrial Research Institute provides technical support by way of food safety and product development services.

2.7.6 Business Support Institutions

Major business support institutions that offer assistance to improve the competitiveness of the hot pepper sauce industry include the Trinidad and Tobago Agribusiness Association, the National Agricultural Marketing and Development Company, the Food and Beverage Industry Development Committee, the Trinidad and Tobago Manufacturing Association, the National Entrepreneurship Development Company Limited and exporTT Limited. These organizations offer a range of services, including local and international networking opportunities, training, and export advice and facilitation.

2.7.7 Financial Institutions

Financial institutions offer savings, investments and loans to facilitate the industry. In addition to the commercial banks, the Agricultural Development Bank, a state agency, focuses on financial solutions for the agribusiness sector. The National Entrepreneurship Development Company Limited, another state-owned company, offers loan financing and grants for start-ups and expansion of micro and small enterprises.

2.7.8 Government and Statutory Agencies

A number of government ministries interact with the hot pepper sauce industry, including the Ministry of Food Production, Land and Marine Affairs,

Ministry of Trade and the Ministry of Health. The Trinidad and Tobago Bureau of Standards provides a number of services, including measuring, laboratory and standards certification.

2.8 Local Industry Conditions

The local hot pepper sauce industry can be analysed by using Porter's diamond model, where demand conditions, factor conditions, firm strategy, structure and rivalry, and related and supporting industries are considered (Porter 1990).

2.8.1 Demand Conditions

There is strong local demand for hot pepper sauce, which is used both as a cooking ingredient and as a table sauce. The local palate for hot pepper sauce is well-developed and requires a range of spice levels, from mild to hot. It is a fundamental feature in the local food service sector, which was valued at US$771.6 million in 2011 (Gonzalez 2012). This sector consists of thirty-eight hundred full-service restaurants, cafes, bars, street stalls and fast-food outlets and has experienced annual growth of 7.8 per cent over the last five years (ibid.).

2.8.2 Factor Conditions

Resources for the hot pepper sauce industry are readily available. However, there is a shortfall in the availability of local hot peppers for the production of pepper mash which is usually supplemented by imported peppers and peppermash. In terms of human resources, Trinidad and Tobago has a total labour force of 611,500 persons. Labour rates are inexpensive – the hourly wage is US$1.95. While the food and beverage industries in Trinidad and Tobago generally have a ready supply of skilled and unskilled labour (Citibank 2011), feedback from industry indicates that there is a skills gap where the labour force is inadequately trained in certain areas (Compete Caribbean 2012).

In terms of energy resources, government subsidies have pushed the cost of electricity down to US$0.03 per kilowatt hour, which is less than one-tenth of the energy costs in other parts of the Caribbean.[3] Hot pepper sauce processors can also access a number of incentives in the form of exemptions from custom duties, value-added tax and income tax for a specified period of time when establishing their businesses. Real estate is also readily available – for example, land and buildings can be leased from Evolving Technologies and Enterprise Development Company, a state organization which manages nineteen industrial parks where physical infrastructure is already in place.

2.9 Firm Strategy, Structure and Rivalry

With the proliferation of hot pepper sauce processors, rivalry in the industry is increasing. Currently, large processors dominate supermarket shelves, with their product offerings consisting of fundamental variety in terms of various hot pepper sauce types, and peripheral variety in the form of different brand names and bottle sizes. The medium and small hot pepper sauce processors also produce a range of offerings. However, unlike the large processors, the medium and small processors focus less on the peripheral variety, instead concentrating on fundamental variety by producing different hot pepper sauce types, using alternative pepper types, and additional fruits and vegetables for special flavours.

2.10 Related and Supporting Institutions

The related and supporting institutions and organizations appear to differentiate their service offerings. On the one hand, services offered by organizations like Food and Beverage Industry Development Committee (export facilitation, training in supply chain management and regional networking opportunities) target the medium and large hot pepper sauce processors. On the other hand, services offered to the small and micro-processors include training in basic processing techniques, food preservation and food safety.

Additionally, many of the supporting organizations that focus on the cottage hot pepper sauce segment promote cooperation among the processors. For example, the Caribbean Network of Rural Women Producers is a regional organization made up of rural women's associations from Barbados, Grenada, St Vincent, St Lucia, Guyana, Suriname, Jamaica, and Trinidad and Tobago. In promoting the hot pepper cottage segment of the hot pepper sauce industry, the Inter-American Institute for Cooperation on Agriculture has facilitated the participation of the Caribbean Network of Rural Women Producers members in workshops related to hot pepper mash production.

2.11 Lessons Learned

There are four main lessons emerging out of the GVC analysis of the Trinidad and Tobago hot pepper sauce industry.

2.11.1 Structure of the Fresh Hot Pepper Cultivation Industry

The local hot pepper industry is characterized by a large number of small farmers, who are dispersed across the country (Iton and Mohammed 2006). Although there is evidence of informal agreements between farmers and small hot pepper sauce producers, there appears to be little cooperation and coordination between the fresh hot pepper farmers and the downstream processors of pepper mash and hot pepper sauce. The absence of formal contractual arrangements contrasts with the situation in competing markets and could partially explain why the Trinidad and Tobago industry has been in decline since 2001. In Costa Rica, for example, the hot pepper industry is characterized by farmer groups that enter into contractual arrangements with the downstream processors – processors even provide input supplies for the growing of the hot peppers, technical assistance, and financing (Caribbean Export Development Agency 2004). The arrangements have the effect of reducing producer risk and incentivizing production, thereby increasing the supply and driving down the cost of locally produced pepper mash. Meanwhile, in Trinidad and Tobago, the local supply is insufficient to meet the demands of the three main markets and has to rely on the import of both fresh hot peppers and pepper mash.

2.11.2 High Cost of Locally Produced Pepper Mash

The cost of local pepper mash is almost twice the cost of the imported product coming from Costa Rica. This result is not surprising since the cost of this intermediate product will reflect the cost of the main raw material. With the declining supply of local fresh hot peppers, the average prices received by local farmers have increased, moving from an average of US$4.84/kilogram in 2010 to US$7.92/kilogram in 2012 (Central Statistical Office of Trinidad and Tobago).

2.11.3 Product Differentiation of Pepper Mash

In many industries, the intermediate product is a commodity item. Differentiation is only introduced in the latter manufacturing stages, when the final product is being produced, thereby allowing for greater value creation and value capture by the final stage manufacturers. In the pepper sauce industry, however, the intermediate product, pepper mash, is not a commodity item. It can be produced in a variety of ways. As a result, hot pepper sauce producers are offered a range of pepper mash to use as the base for their final products, classified by pepper types, flavours and degree of hotness. These differences account for price variance in the cost of pepper mash – for example, Louisiana Pepper Exchange produces eight different types of pepper mash by pepper type, and further differentiation can be specified by the buyer in terms of salt and vinegar content.

2.11.4 Contract Manufacturing of Hot Pepper Sauce

There are a number of private label manufacturers that produce and package hot pepper sauce for food companies, supermarket chains, food distributors and other private brand owners. These private label manufacturers offer a full range of services, including the research and development of hot pepper sauce recipes onto processing and packaging. Alimentos Kámuk is a private label manufacturer that operates in Costa Rica, with customers in North America, Central America and the Caribbean, South America, Europe and Africa.

As with other manufacturing industries, the use of contract manufacturing or outsourcing of production activities in the pepper sauce industry is a noteworthy trend. Contract manufacturers, because of their production capacity and their ability to perform quick changeovers, can compete on the basis of flexibility and provide their customers with products that meet a wide range of specifications. While outsourcing is a complex manufacturing strategy decision, it provides companies with the option of focusing on higher value-added activities such as research and development, and branding and promotional activities. Once the total cost of outsourcing allows for a company to realize an acceptable profit margin, contract manufacturing is a viable business model to pursue.

2.12 Upgrading Strategies for the Local Hot Pepper Sauce Industry

Drawing on the previous analysis, the Trinidad and Tobago hot pepper sauce industry displays a number of elements that point to opportunities for its greater participation in GVCs. In addition to having a well-established sector that spans the entire chain, there is a mix of capabilities that can allow for different actors to target diverse market opportunities.

Three types of upgrading in the hot pepper sauce industry are recommended, based on the GVC methodology: product upgrading, expansion into pepper mash manufacturing, and end marketing upgrading. Product upgrading relates to moving into more sophisticated product lines, expansion along the chain includes initiating activities in multiple stages of the chain, and market upgrading relates to moving into new markets (Gereffi and Fernandez-Stark 2011). These are discussed below.

Internationally, demand for "fiery foods" has led to the incorporation of hot sauces in a variety of other products, including condiments and sauces, snack foods, and ready-to-eat meals. The "fiery foods" product line therefore represents opportunities for the Trinidad and Tobago hot pepper industry – large- and medium-sized hot pepper sauce manufacturers can use hot sauces to create new products in their condiments and sauce lines.

2.12.1 Expansion into Pepper Mash Manufacturing

Pepper mash manufacturing is a high-demand activity based on the increasing number of hot pepper sauce processors and their demand for this intermediate good. For the local industry, the manufacture of pepper mash is an opportunity for greater participation in the value chain. The hot pepper varieties grown in Trinidad and Tobago present prospects for specialized West Indian flavours of pepper mash that can be sold to the pepper sauce processors. Similarly, there are opportunities for local companies to contract manufacturers for private labels. As Trinidad and Tobago labour costs are higher than those of competitors such as Costa Rica, local manufacturers can focus on niche segments such as leveraging their competitive strengths of blending and creating flavours.

2.12.2 End Market Upgrading

There are opportunities for the local hot pepper industry to enter non-traditional markets. Currently, export is concentrated on markets where there are large Caribbean diaspora populations (New York, Miami, London, Toronto). Yet with the growing popularity of hot pepper sauces, there are opportunities for local manufacturers to target new markets where Trinidad and Tobago's hot pepper sauce flavours branded on "Caribbean island mystic" can present different and exotic taste options.

2.13 Recommendations

The local hot pepper sauce industry has a well-established value chain with full participation in all of the activities. Based on the deficiencies identifed in section 2.6, three policy recommendations have emerged from the GVC analysis of the industry.

2.13.1 Policy Recommendations for Insufficient Local Supply

The insufficient local supply of fresh hot peppers limits the hot pepper sauce industry, so the volume of fresh hot peppers supplied needs to be increased, particularly since the country's hot pepper varieties provide it with an important competitive advantage. Two policy recommendations are outlined as follows:

1. In terms of quantity of supply, the Ministry of Food Production has a number of incentives to stimulate the agricultural sector and has targeted traditional crops such as citrus, cocoa, coffee and coconuts.[4] Since hot peppers have been identifed as a targeted non-traditional crop, the policy recommendation is that hot peppers should be included in the ministry's incentive programme.
2. The ministry has also implemented the Commercial Large Farms Programmes to increase the quantity of locally cultivated crops. The policy recommendation is that a certain acreage should be reserved for growing hot peppers.

2.13.2 Recommendation for the Structure of Local Industry

There is little coordination between small local farmers and actors in the downstream segments of the chain, which means that mash producers cannot depend on the reliability of the local supply. The following policy recommendation is designed to address this challenge and increase local reliability: Via the business support organizations, the coordination of the hot pepper industry can be formalized by the use of contractual arrangements. For instance, hot pepper farmers can be organized into cooperatives to contractually supply downstream processors.

2.14 Conclusion

These policy recommendations seek to increase the quantity and reliability of the supply of fresh hot peppers. By increasing the quantity and reliability of raw material supplies, the hot pepper sauce industry will be able to leverage the range of hot pepper varieties grown in Trinidad and Tobago, thereby engaging in functional upgrading opportunities via the production of a range of pepper mash mixtures and the production of hot pepper sauces for private labels through contract manufacturing. The stability of local raw material supply would also allow for large processors to engage in product upgrading via the expansion of their product lines into the "fiery foods" segments. It would also enhance the stability of the finished stocks of pepper sauce manufacturers engaged in end market upgrading, via entry into non-traditional markets.

Available trade data shows that increasing local production of hot pepper would augur well for the local hot pepper industry, benefiting local actors who engage in supplying fresh or chilled hot peppers to local processors as well as local actors who export fresh or chilled hot peppers. According to the International Trade Centre, from 2010 to 2014 imports of fresh or chilled pepper to Trinidad and Tobago decreased from US$390,000 to US$164,000, while in the simultaneous time period, world imports of fresh or chilled peppers increased from US$4.185 billion to US$5.017 billion. Similarly, from 2010 to 2014, exports of fresh or chilled peppers from Trinidad and Tobago declined from US$570,000 to US$281,000, while world exports increased from US$4.061 billion to US$4.797 billion (www.trademap.org). By increasing local pepper supply to the production levels achieved in the early 2000s, Trinidad and Tobago would create increased opportunities for stronger participation in the hot pepper GVC.

Notes

1. Hot peppers or chillis are part of the genus Capsicum, which comprises five domesticated species: Capsicum Annuum (includes jalapeño variety), Capsicum Frutescens (includes tabasco variety), Capsicum Chinense (includes habanero and Scotch bonnet varieties), Capsicum Baccatum and Capsicum Pubescens (Pino, Sauri-Duch and Marbot 2006).
2. For general background on hot pepper sauce production, please see the appendix to case study 2.

3. Electricity tariffs range from TTD$0.1450 to TT$0.2180 for industrial customers, and TTD$0.4150 to TT$0.61 for commercial customers. https://ttec.co.tt/services/tariffs/default.htm#commercial, accessed 10 November 2014 (TTD$1 = USD$0.15 as of 23 June 2016).
4. The Ministry of Food Production's incentive programme is detailed in http://agriculture.gov.tt/images/AIP_Brochures/Agricultural%20Incentive%20Programme%202011.pdf, and targets citrus, cocoa, coffee and coconut crop establishment and rehabilitation. Other incentives include complete or partial funding for vehicle, machinery and equipment purchases, installation of irrigation infrastructure, and land preparation and soil conservation activities.

References

Bosland, P., D. Coon, and G. Reeves. 2012. "'Trinidad Moruga Scorpion' Pepper is the World's Hottest Measured Chile Pepper at More Than Two Million Scoville Heat Units". *HortTechnology* 22 (4): 534–38. http://www.chilepepperinstitute.org/content/files/trinidad_moruga_scorpion_pepper_hottest.pdf.

CARDI (Caribbean Agricultural Research and Development Institute). 2011. "Trinidad and Tobago Unit: Highlights of Research and Development Interventions". Accessed 18 July 2013. http://www.cardi.org/wp-content/uploads/2011/02/CARDI-TT-UNIT-ACHIEVEMENTS-_8.9.2011-JL_.pdf.

Caribbean Export Development Agency. 2004. *Hot Pepper Project Phase 1: Market Research on the Viability and Export Potential of the Regional Hot Pepper Industry*. Brittons Hill, Barbados: Caribbean Export Agency.

Chile Pepper Institute. 2005. "2004 World Chile Production Statistics". *Chile Pepper Institute Newsletter* 16, no. 3 (Fall): 1–2. http://www.chilepepperinstitute.org/content/files/05%20fall.pdf.

Citibank. 2011. "Trinidad and Tobago Investment Guide 2011–2012". Accessed 30 July 2013. http://www.latam.citibank.com/corporate/trinidad/common/pdf/CitibankInvestmentGuide.pdf.

Compete Caribbean. 2012. "Trinidad and Tobago Enterprise Survey Country Bulletin". *Compete Caribbean*. Accessed 29 July 2013. http://www.competecaribbean.org/category/surveys.

Gereffi, G., and K. Fernandez-Stark. 2011. *Global Value Chain Analysis: A Primer*. Durham, NC: Duke University Center on Globalization, Governance and Competitiveness. http://www.cggc.duke.edu/pdfs/2011-05-31_GVC_analysis_a_primer.pdf.

Gonzalez, O. 2012. "Caribbean Basin Food Service: Hotel Restaurant Institutional – Trinidad and Tobago Food Service Sector Report". 27 April. Accessed 30 July 2013. https://s3.amazonaws.com/ProductionContentBucket/pdf/20120513184838932.pdf.

GORTT (Government of the Republic of Trinidad and Tobago). 2013. "Review of the Economy 2012: Stimulating Growth, Generating Prosperity". Accessed 12 July 2013. http://www.finance.gov.tt/content/Review-of-the-Economy-2012.pdf.

Iton, A., and A. Mohammed. 2006. "Marketing of Trinidad and Tobago's Hot Peppers". *Caribbean Argiculture Research and Development Institute.* Accessed 1 July 2013. http://www.cardi.org/wp-content/uploads/downloads/2012/11/MARKETING-OF-TRINIDAD-AND-TOBAGO-Hot-Pepper-Final-Jul-07.pdf.

Liu, Y., and M. Nair. 2010. "Non-pungent Functional Food Components in the Water Extracts of Hot Peppers". *Food Chemistry* 122, no. 3: 731–36.

Meléndez, M., and M. Uribe. 2012. International Product Fragmentation and the Insertion of LAC in Global Production Networks: Columbian Case Studies. Washington, DC: Inter-American Development Bank. http://services.iadb.org/wmsfiles/products/Publications/37694000.pdf.

Ministry of Food Production, Land and Marine Affairs. 2012. "The National Food Production Action Plan 2012–2015". Accessed 1 May 2013. http://www.agriculture.gov.tt/pdf/National%20Food%20Production%20Action%20Plan%202012-2015.pdf.

NOU Magazine. 2000. "The Promise of Peppers". Accessed 1 March 2013. http://kiwi-life.ifp3.com/root/Kiwi-Life/files/THE%20PROMISE%20OF%20PEPPERS1.pdf.

Pino, J., E Sauri-Duch and R. Marbot. 2006. "Changes in Volatile Compounds of Habanero Chile Pepper (Capsicum Chinense Jack cv. Habanero) at Two Ripening Stages". *Food Chemistry* 94: 394–98.

Porter, M. 1990. "The Competitive Advantage of Nations". *Harvard Business Review* (March–April): 73–93.

Richardson, M. 2012. "Hot Stuff: Louisiana Pepper Exchange Makes the Mash for Spicy Condiments". 3 April. Accessed 1 July 2013. http://businessreport.com/article/20120430/BUSINESSREPORT0401/304309986.

Tully and Holland. 2010. "Condiments and Sauces Industry Update". October. Accessed 12 July 2013. http://www.tullyandholland.com/UploadedFiles/Publications/Condiments&SaucesIndustryUpdate-October2010-KGirb-MnVQs-iqJOp.pdf.

Appendix 2.1 Background to Hot Pepper Sauce Industry

Hot pepper sauce, also referred to as hot sauce, pepper sauce and spicy chilli sauce, falls within the condiments, sauces and dressings industry, and serves as a cooking and marinating ingredient, as well as a table sauce and dip. There are numerous types of hot pepper sauces, which are mainly differentiated by the type, blend and proportion of hot peppers used as one of the major raw materials, the addition of other ingredients for preserving, flavouring and colouring the sauce, and the processing method. Hot pepper sauces are therefore often classified by the main type of hot pepper used, such as jalapeño, chipotle and habanero peppers.

Since the choice of ingredients and processing styles is often based on traditions specific to particular locations, pepper sauce types are also classified by place of origin, such as American Louisiana-style hot sauce, Thai hot sauce and West Indian pepper sauce. Hot pepper sauces are also classified based on the degree of intensity, as measured by the Scoville Heat Index, which ranges from zero to over 1 million units. Hot pepper sauces therefore range from extremely mild to extremely hot.

In addition to the hot pepper sauce type, branding is another key feature in this industry. Brands range from well-established internationally known brands, to regional brands that are famous in specific areas, to private labels of distributors such as large supermarket chains, to the little known brands of small entrepreneurs who operate in the micro hot pepper sauce industry.

CASE STUDY 3

The Rum Industry of Guyana in the Global Value Chain

DIANNA DaSILVA-GLASGOW
PhD Student
Sir Arthur Lewis Institute of Social and Economic Studies
University of the West Indies, St Augustine

LOUIS DODSON
Public Policy Consultant
Citizen Security Programme
Ministry of Home Affairs, Guyana

Abstract

This case study examines the firm-specific and local factors responsible for Guyana's sustained rum export success. The study uses the global value chain (GVC) framework and primary and secondary data to conduct studies of the global and local markets. The key finding of the study is that the maturity and capacity of the rum industry for consistent exports, in both the bulk and premium niche segments of the market, is linked to maintaining quality through investments in international standards compliance and through continuously upgrading productive capacity by investing in human capital and physical infrastructure. In light of challenges presently faced on the international market, the study suggests upgrading in the branded niche segment and offers policy recommendations for sustaining the industry's competitiveness in that segment.

3.1 Introduction

Guyana is one of the most open economies in the Caribbean region. However, the country has an undiversified export base consisting of products mainly from the agriculture and extractive industries. The main export commodities are sugar, gold, bauxite, shrimp, timber and rice. Combined, these goods account for nearly 60 per cent of the country's gross domestic product (CIA 2014).

Despite its abundant resources, domestic value creation through manufacturing has been minimal.

While Guyana's manufacturing capacity remains limited, the country has been involved in the successful exportation of rum for decades. The rum manufacturing industry in Guyana started in the sixteenth century. Over the years, the sector has evolved to such an extent that rum producers compete in the premium global rum market on the basis of quality. The experience of this industry offers useful lessons for other sectors that are seeking to enhance capacity to compete in the global market.

The objective of this study is to identify and examine the firm-specific, industry and national-level factors that are responsible for Guyana's sustained export of rum while also assessing potential challenges and the possibility of upgrading. This is done using the GVC framework and includes a step-by-step study of the global market juxtaposed with the local market for rum. Data for the study was obtained through interviews with company representatives, international statistical databases such as the United Nations Commodity Trade Statistics Database and Datamonitor, national documents and company annual reports.

The rest of the study is structured as follows:

- Section 3.2 outlines the input-output structure of the rum GVC.
- Section 3.3 analyses key trends for the global supply and demand of rum and identifies the major players in the industry.
- Section 3.4 assesses the local context of Guyana's participation in the rum GVC.
- Section 3.5 analyses the competitiveness of Guyana's rum industry.
- Section 3.6 examines the main roles of the primary and secondary stakeholders and their levels of importance and influence.
- Section 3.7 analyses the upgrading strategies and tactics pursued by rum producers and examines further upgrading opportunities.
- Section 3.8 outlines lessons learned from the industry analysis.
- Sections 3.9 and 3.10 outline policy recommendations and key conclusions.

3.2 Input-Output Structure of the Rum Global Value Chain

The rum GVC encompasses five stages (see figure 3.1). It starts with the production of sugar cane and sugar cane by-products. The West Indies Rum and Spirits

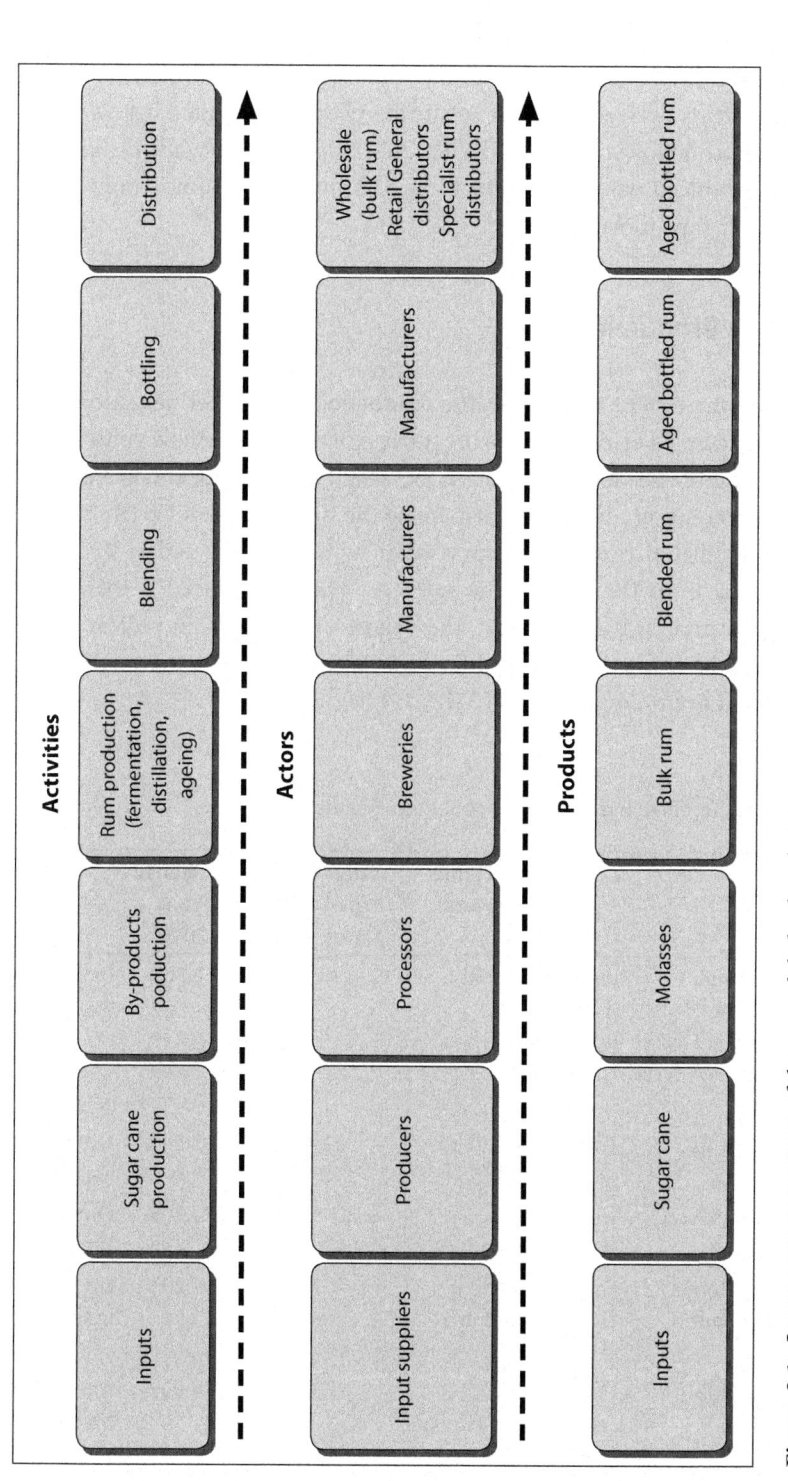

Figure 3.1. Input-output structure of the rum global value chain

Association (WIRSPA) defines rum as "any spirit distilled solely from the fermented sugars derived from the sugarcane plant and distilled below ninety-six per cent alcohol by volume" (WIRSPA 2013b). Therefore, while distilled spirits can be produced using by-products such as juice, true rum is only produced from sugar cane molasses.

3.3 Rum Production

There are three steps involved in the production of rum: fermentation, distillation and ageing. Fermentation is the process of adding specially cultivated yeast to diluted molasses to produce a "wash", which then produces cogeners such as acids and compounds that in turn create the distilled spirit (WIRSPA 2013b). At the distillation stage, the heavy water content (estimated at 93 per cent) is removed from the "wash". The spirit or "mark" produced is then matured through a process called ageing. The degree of ageing is an indication of the quality of the spirit. Therefore, older rums usually have a better quality and are considered premium spirits (WIRSPA 2013b).

Table 3.1. Top Five Best-Selling Global Rum Brands, 2011

Brand	Company Name (Headquarters)	Sales 2011 (Mn of 9-litre Cases Sold)	% Change from 2010	Status
Bacardi Rum (Other brands: Don Q, Ron Del Barrilito, Destileria Coqui)	Bacardi Limited (Hamilton, Bermuda)	19.28	+3.70%	International brand
Tanduay Rhum	Tanduay Distillers (Manila, Philippines)	18.36	+8.50%	Domestic/local
McDowell's No.1 Celebration	United Spirits (Bangalore, India)	13.89	+24.40%	Domestic/local
Captain Morgan Original Spiced Rum	Diageo (London, United Kingdom)	8.70	+1.20%	International brand
Havana Club	Havana Club International (Cuba/France)	3.77	+14.90%	International brand

Source: Drinks International Millionaires Club Report 2011.

The colour of rum is linked to the container in which it is aged. In the Caribbean, especially Guyana, oak barrels are used to age rums, giving them a brown hue as the rum takes the natural colour of the barrel (caramel can also be added to darken the rum). Clear rums are aged in steel containers. There are several classifications of rum based on colour and texture: white rums, golden/amber rums, dark rums, spiced rums, rum punches and premium rums (WIRSPA 2013b).

Most rum producers have vertically integrated rum production operations (fermentation, distillation and ageing). This is because each stage contributes to the manufacturer's capacity to produce unique varieties of rums and acquire brand recognition. Table 3.1 shows the top selling brands worldwide, based on sales. Puerto Rican Bacardi is the dominant brand globally, selling 19.3 million cases in 2010.

3.4 Blending

The rum produced up to the ageing stage is "bulk rum". It is sometimes blended by adding various spices in order to produce a unique flavour and aroma. Various rum varieties, by age and flavour, can also be blended together. Blending may be done within a firm that also undertakes fermentation, distillation and ageing as an additional aspect of rum production, or it may be undertaken by entirely different firms that purchase bulk rum from other producers.

3.5 Bottling

After rum is blended, it is then bottled. Bottling can be done by specialty firms or by the manufacturers of bulk rum. Rum can be blended and bottled in areas that are not major rum producers such as Austria, Newfoundland, Tennessee, Germany and the Netherlands. Rum can also be aged in locations where it is not produced. In Canada for instance, rums from Antigua, Barbados and Jamaica are imported and aged for five years then branded locally as Screech (Whiskey Exchange 2014).

3.6 Distribution

From an economic standpoint, the high weight-to-value ratio of bottled rum points to the advantage of bottling rum close to the market where it is consumed.

Most often, rum is distributed as bulk rum before it is blended and bottled at a second location. Bottled rum is also dispersed by general distributors or specialist rum distributors. The travel retail channel is a noteworthy avenue through which rums are sold globally. In 2012, this channel accounted for 5 per cent of total spirits sales globally (Pernod Ricard 2013).

3.7 Global Supply and Demand for Rum

3.7.1 Leading Suppliers of Rum and Their Competitive Strengths

In the global industry, the Caribbean and Latin America are regarded as the epicentre of rum production.[1] In the premium end of the market, however, it is multinational corporations that predominate. These corporations are mostly based in developed countries, with operations and partnerships in several countries, including developing nations. For instance, Diageo London operates twenty-seven production facilities, including distillation and bottling facilities in Scotland, Italy, France, Spain, Germany, England, Puerto Rico and Mexico, among others. As depicted in table 3.2, Captain Morgan Original Spiced Rum (Diageo London) and Havana Club (Pernod Ricard, Paris) are headquartered in developed countries (the United Kingdom and France, respectively), but have operations across several developing countries. Captain Morgan, for instance, operates in several Latin American and Caribbean markets, employing about eighteen hundred people. In fact, some 20 per cent of the 19 million cases of rum supplied to the Latin American and Caribbean markets are produced within the region itself through third-party suppliers (Diageo 2014).

The companies that are leading suppliers of rum globally are identified in table 3.2 above. These firms have become successful by implementing a number of strategies, including branding, vertically integrating operations, outsourcing, investing in multiple strategic markets and differentiating production techniques. These strategies are discussed further in the following sections.

3.7.2 Branding

Branding has been an important strategy for firms in the global rum industry to reach international customers and expand market share. For instance, Pernod Ricard has pointedly stated that its strategy is based on brand upscaling; as a result, it spends 19 per cent of net sales on marketing (Pernod Ricard 2013).

Table 3.2. Leading Rum Producers Worldwide, 2014

Company name (headquarters)	Revenue (US$bn)	Assets (US$bn)	Number of employees	Global Presence (Number of Countries)	Number of Distilleries/ Production Sites	Leading Brand	Markets
Bacardi Limited Hamilton (Bermuda)	5 (est. 2012)	3.6	4,000	16	27	Bacardi Rum	United States 41% Europe 30% Australia 14% Other 15%
Tanduay Distillers (Manila, Philippines)	0.008	7.0	1,508	0		Tanduay Rhum	Mainly local, exports account for 0.1% of share but key markets include Hong Kong, United States and United Arab Emirates
United Spirits Ltd (Bangalore, India)	1.4	1.7	7,500	0	26	McDowell's No.1 Celebration	Mainly local but also Africa, the Far East and India
Diageo (London, United Kingdom)	24.5	28.6	28,000	11	30	Johnnie Walker, Captain Morgan	North America 34% Western Europe 21% Africa, Eastern Europe and Turkey 21% Latin America and Caribbean 11% Asia Pacific 13%
Pernod Ricard (Paris, France)	9.6	34.4	18,972	23	–	Havana Club	Asia and rest of the world 38% Americas 27% Europe 35%

Sources: Tanduay Holdings Annual Report 2013; Bacardi Annual Report 2013; United Spirits Annual Report 2013; Diageo Annual Report 2013/2014; Pernod Ricard Annual Report 2012/2013.

Table 3.3. Top Ten Rum Brands in Europe ('000s of 9-litre cases)

Brand	Owner	Volume 2007	Volume 2010	Volume 2011	% change 2011 on 2010	5-year % CAGR
Bacardi	Bacardi-Martini	5,206.6	4,778.7	4,968.1	4.0	−1.3
Havana Club	Pernod Ricard	1,717.4	2,049.1	2,092.6	2.1	6.4
Captain Morgan	Diageo	575.9	1,216.3	1,588.0	30.6	25.9
Brugal	Edrington Group	1,024.8	1,073.2	939.5	−12.5	1.9
Bozkov	Stock Spirits	753.5	723.0	887.5	22.8	4.6
Negrita	La Martiniquaise	686.3	900.0	881.0	−2.1	5.8
Barceló	Barceló	516.7	801.0	842.3	5.1	14.1
Old Nick	La Martiniquaise	179.0	352.0	400.5	13.8	22.5
Cacique	Diageo	1,088.4	674.2	396.8	−41.1	−19.3
Pampero	Diageo	473.1	420.9	396.4	−5.8	−2.2
Total		**12,221.7**	**12,988.4**	**13,392.7**	**3.1**	

Source: *International Wine and Spirits Record*, November 2012.

Table 3.3 looks at the top ten European global brands (in volume terms) and their level of penetration in the European rum market.

Of the ten, Bacardi, a brand of Bacardi-Martini (a 152-year-old family-owned company), sold the highest amount of rum in 2011. Diageo and La Martiniquaise accounted for three and two of the top ten brands, respectively. However, of Diageo's three brands, only Captain Morgan shows a positive and relatively high (26 per cent) five-year compound annual growth rate.

Bacardi-Martini's and Diageo's rums are also among the top ten brands in the US market for spirits, with sales volumes of over 8 and 6 million cases in 2011, respectively (*International Wine and Spirits Record*, August 2012). However, the compound annual growth rates for both brands for the period 2006–2011 are −0.8 and 1.5, which means that while Bacardi-Martini has the top rum brand in both Europe and the United States, it has also recorded negative compound annual growth rates in both markets. Therefore, its challenge, like all other dominant product brands, is to maintain market share. In North America, Bacardi's market share dropped marginally over the last decade from 25 per cent to 21 per cent in 2012 (ibid.).

In contrast to Bacardi-Martini and Diageo, both of La Martiniquaise's brands reported positive five-year compound annual growth rates, with Old Nick reporting a relatively high 22.5 per cent rate of growth over a five-year period (see table 3.3). The eighty-year-old France-based company, which began importing rum from the French colony of Martinique in 1936 (*International Wine and Spirits Record*, November 2012), runs twenty-four production sites in France, Scotland and Spain where it distils and blends La Martiniquaise rums. The company is vertically integrated and has a presence in most segments of the rum GVC. In the 1960s, La Martiniquaise made the strategic decision to align itself with off-premise distribution in French supermarkets such as Carrefour and Leclerc (ibid.). This focus on supermarkets and, increasingly, discount stores, remains important for the company today.

Finally, Barceló's five-year compound annual growth rate of 14 per cent is the third highest among the top ten brands in Europe. The eighty-four-year-old company has market shares in the United States, Canada, Mexico, France, Germany, Italy, and Russia (Barceló 2014). Like its Dominican counterpart, Brugal, it is a dominant player in the Spanish rum market – together, these two companies accounted for a third of rum sales (WIRSPA 2013a). Like other top companies, Barceló is also active in each of the several stages of the rum GVC (Barceló 2014).

Through branding, firms can use different products to enter targeted markets. For instance, Bacardi created the D'ussé Cognac XO brand in the United States to appeal to the luxury segment of the market (Pardis Cognac 2014). Diageo also has a significant presence in the Brazilian market through its Johnnie Walker brand – Brazil is the number one market worldwide for the Johnnie Walker Red Label (Diageo n.d.).

3.7.3 Vertically Integrated Operations

Most rum producers have vertically integrated operations where they perform distillation, fermentation, ageing, blending, bottling and distribution. Each stage has an effect on the characteristics of the final product, which allows manufacturers to acquire brand recognition. Vertically integrating operations is therefore a way of exerting greater control over the quality of rum produced.

Additionally, since rum has a substantial weight-to-value ratio, many leading suppliers decide to locate in specific markets so that warehouses and distribution outlets are closer to end markets (Diageo 2014).

3.7.4 Outsourcing

While a number of firms tend to have vertically integrated operations that span the entire value chain, many companies do outsource some aspects of

Table 3.4. Investments by Key Rum-Producing Firms

Company	Market of Investment	Nature of Investment	Year
Diageo	India	Diageo bought 27.4 per cent share in United Spirits group for $2.04bn. (now 53.4 per cent)	2012
Edrington Group	Dominican Republic	The Edrington Group, a large Scottish distilling company, acquired 60 per cent of Brugal and Company.	2008
Fortune		Fortune acquired Cruzan from Pernod Ricard for US$100m	2008
Diageo		Diageo acquired the global distribution rights to Zacapa	2008
CL Financial	Jamaica	CL Financial, which owns Angostura rum, acquired Lascelles deMercado and Company, producer of the Appleton Rum brand, for around $900m	2008
Tanduay Distillers Inc.		Tandauay Distillers Inc. acquired 90 per cent of Asian Alcohol Corp (now 95 per cent) and Absolut Chemicals Inc. (now 96 per cent)	2005
Havana Club	Cuba	Since 1994 it has been produced by Havana Club International, a 50:50 joint venture between Pernod Ricard and the Cuban government	1994
Bacardi Ltd		Bacardi-Martini is a subsidiary group of Bacardi Ltd. It acquired Martini and Rossi to form Bacardi-Martini	1993

Sources: http://www.diageo.com/en-row/investor/Pages/FAQs.aspx, http://en.wikipedia.org/wiki/Havana_Club, http://tanduay.com/subsidiaries.html, http://en.wikipedia.org/wiki/Brugal, http://www.bbc.com/news/business-20267619, Just Drinks (2009); http://en.wikipedia.org/wiki/Bacardi

production or distribution to third parties through joint ventures and other contract arrangements. Eighty per cent of Diageo's rum production occurs through its own facilities located in the United States, Canada, Ireland and the United Kingdom, but 20 per cent is outsourced to commercial partners across several markets (Diageo 2014). Some firms may purchase bulk rum from producers and undertake ageing and blending. This is popular in Europe's rum market, where companies in France, the United Kingdom and Germany blend, age and bottle bulk rums imported from the Caribbean.

3.7.5 Investments in Multiple Strategic Markets

Investments by leading multinational firms are transforming the nature of rum production from a cottage industry base to a concentrated sector led by a few multinational firms (Cooper 2009). Globally, rum production is more consolidated as leading firms have sought to undertake investments in multiple markets as a way of building brands and securing global positions (Just Drinks 2009) (see table 3.4). For instance, Diageo acquired a 27.4 per cent share in United Spirits of India in 2012 to position the company to take advantage of the growing Indian market (BBC News 2012).

A notable characteristic of these investments is that companies from developed countries are targeting firms based in developing nations. For instance, the Edrington group, a Scottish distilling company, acquired 60 per cent of Brugal and Company in the Dominican Republic in 2008.

3.8 Market Segments

Table 3.5 shows the market segments where leading firms earn revenues. For instance, white rum accounts for 28 per cent of Pernod Ricard's sales. For Tanduay Distillers, 76 per cent of revenues come from the sale of dark rums.

3.9 Global Trends

Global demand for rum reached US$2.8 billion in 2012 (author's calculation based on ITC, n.d.). Approximately 146.4 million cases of rum are sold annually (Just Drinks 2013). While developing countries stand out as producers,

Table 3.5. Market Segment in which Major Firms Operate

Company Name (Headquarters)	Market Segment	End Market
Bacardi Limited (Hamilton, Bermuda)	White rum (Jack Daniels)	–
Tanduay Distillers (Manila, Philippines)	Dark rums account for 74 per cent of sales and 76 per cent of revenues	Standard/economy end
United Spirits Ltd (Bangalore, India)	Dark rums (McDowell's No.1 Celebration is the world's largest dark rum)	–
Diageo (London, United Kingdom)	White and spiced (Johnny Walker and Captain Morgan)	Operate at all price points but mainly premium
Pernod Ricard (Paris, France)	White rums (28 per cent of total market)	Premium

Source: Annual reports of firms.

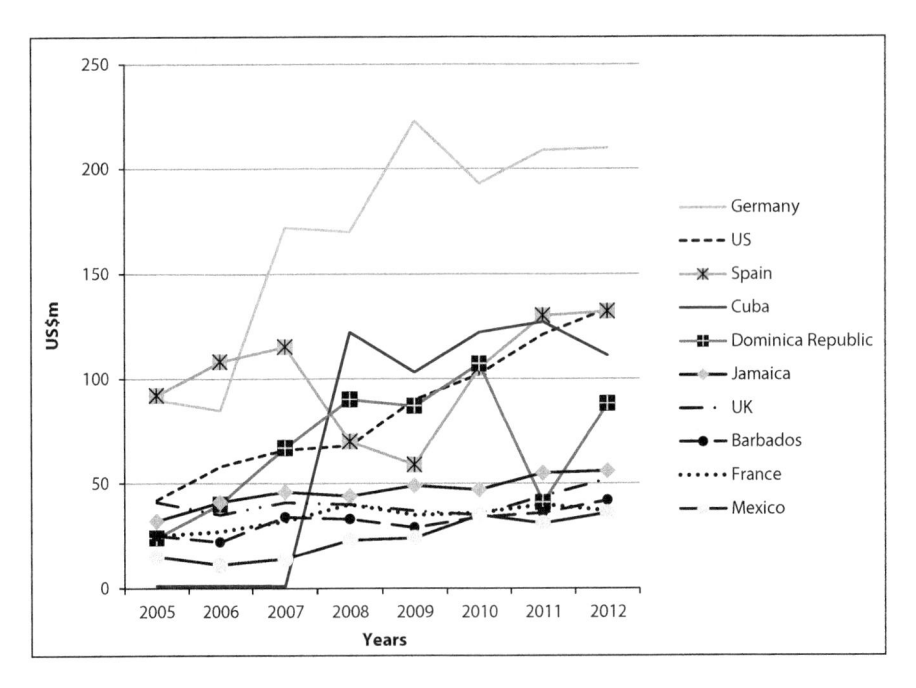

Figure 3.2. Top fifteen exporters of rum, 2005–2012

Source: International Trade Centre calculations based on UN COMTRADE statistics

developed markets account for 61 per cent of global consumption of alcohol (Diageo 2014). Leading brand Havana Club's major markets are Spain, France, Greece and Russia (Just Drinks 2009). Diageo (2014), on the other hand, identifies the US market as its most profitable market.

Figures 3.2 and 3.3 depict the top fifteen export and import markets for rum. The top two importing and exporting countries are Germany and Spain. This trend is explained by the fact that companies such as Pott, Aguilar Import Export (Germany) and Destilerias Arehucas, SA (Spain) import a lot of bulk rum that is re-exported after value-adding.

Spain and Germany show moderate growth rates in imports between 2005 and 2008 before dipping in 2009. In Spain, for example, figure 3.3 shows that imports fell from US$330 million in 2008 to US$256 million in 2009, a drop of 22.4 per cent. It rebounded in 2010 to US$376 million before plummeting again to US$264 million in 2012 (a decline of 30 per cent from 2010).

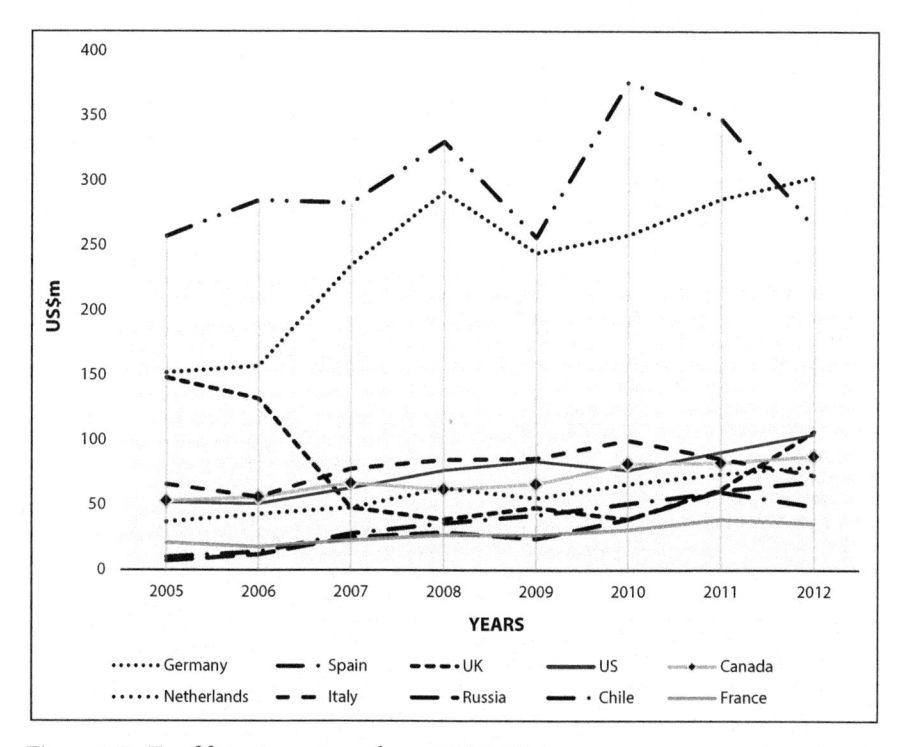

Figure 3.3. Top fifteen importers of rum, 2005–2012
Source: International Trade Centre calculations based on UN COMTRADE statistics.

74 DaSilva-Glasgow and Dodson

Not captured in the import trends above is the demand by India, which is touted as being the largest rum market in the world in volume terms, accounting for about 362 million litres in 2009 (Top 5 of Anything 2014). However, much of this is locally sourced through United Spirits Limited which has about a 59 per cent share of the Indian market (United Spirits n.d.).

Future growth in the rum market seems to be driven by emerging markets. For instance, in 2010 the Indian, Venezuelan, Argentinian and Russian markets grew by 13, 16, 17 and 19 per cent, respectively (Pernod Ricard 2013). The rum market is projected to grow by 7.3 per cent by 2017, and the Asian market alone by 30 per cent (Winchester Capital Research 2014).

3.10 Assessing Guyana's Participation in the Rum Global Value Chain

Figure 3.4 illustrates Guyana's participation in the rum GVC. As can be seen, the country is active in every stage of the chain. However, the local value chain is characterized by the dominance of a few firms.

The state-owned Guyana Sugar Corporation monopolizes sugar production, from which molasses is a by-product. At the rum production stage, there are just two firms – Banks DIH Limited and Demerara Distillers Limited (DDL). Both are large firms with diversified operations producing a range of both alcoholic and non-alcoholic beverages. Banks DIH has fifteen hundred employees and DDL has twelve hundred employees (Banks DIH 2012; DDL 2012).

DDL is the larger of the two rum producers, both with respect to the range of and quantity of products produced. In fact, DDL is the only company actually

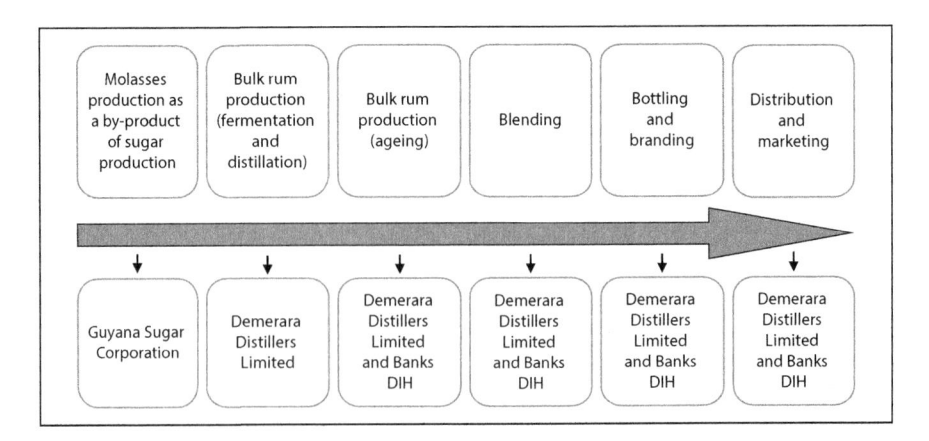

Figure 3.4. Guyana's participation in the rum global value chain

distilling alcohol in Guyana. Seventy per cent of the company's sales come from the production of rum. With a capacity to produce in excess of 26 million litres of pure alcohol annually, it is also the largest supplier of bulk rums and alcohols from the Caribbean to brand owners in Europe and North America (DDL 2012). DDL's client list includes companies such as Diageo, Jim Beam, Hiram Walker, Allied Distillers and Corby's.

Apart from bulk rum production and exports, branding has been an important marketing strategy for DDL. The company has been able to successfully produce and export premium dark aged rums under the flagship brand, El Dorado. DDL spent US$26,000 in 2011 to acquire the El Dorado trademark in the United States and Europe and now produces a range of rums under the brand, including a premium line that was launched in 1992. Evidence of the quality of the spirits is reflected in the numerous international awards it has won – in excess of one hundred international awards, including seven gold awards for its El Dorado brand of rums at the International Wine and Spirits Competition held annually in London ("El Dorado Rums Sweep International Awards", *Kaieteur News*, 9 August 2013). Banks DIH has also won international awards at the International Wine and Spirits Competition (Banks DIH n.d.).

Table 3.6. Subsidiaries and Associates of Demerara Distillers Limited

Company	Country of Registration	Main Business
Distribution Services Ltd	Guyana	Distribution
Demerara Distillers (TT) Ltd	Trinidad	Distribution
Demerara Distillers (US) Inc	United States	Distribution
Demerara Distillers (St Kitts–Nevis) Ltd	St Kitts	Manufacturing and distribution
Breitenstein Holdings BV	Netherlands	Distribution
Demerara Distillers (Europe)	Netherlands	
Breitenstein Trading BV	Netherlands	
MC Murdo Distillers Ltd	United Kingdom	
Demerara Distillers (UK) Ltd	United Kingdom	
Caribbean Distillers Ltd	United Kingdom	
Macleod Distillers Ltd	United Kingdom	
Demerara Rum Company Inc	Canada	Logistics and debt collection agency
Demerara Distillers Limited – Hyderabad	India	Manufacturing and distribution

Source: DDL Annual Report 2012.

DDL's niche in the dark aged rum segment of the market is linked directly to the fact that the company ages its rum in wooden oak barrels. Banks DIH imports bulk rum from Barbados for ageing, blending, bottling and labelling, distribution and marketing under the XM (white rum) label.

Both Banks DIH and DDL are directly involved in marketing the rum they produce. DDL does this through its global subsidiaries and associates in Europe, North America, Asia and the Caribbean (see table 3.6). It also owns 33 per cent of the share capital of National Rums of Jamaica Limited and has a manufacturing and distribution company in Hyderabad, India (DDL 2012). Membership in WIRSPA has played an important role in improving the marketability and distribution of Guyanese rum. WIRSPA has created and launched the Authentic Caribbean Rums distinction as a way of emphasizing the authenticity and quality of imported Caribbean rums.

3.11 Production and Export Trends

In 2012, Guyana produced approximately 20 million litres of rum (see figure 3.5), a marginal decline from previous years. While both bulk and bottled

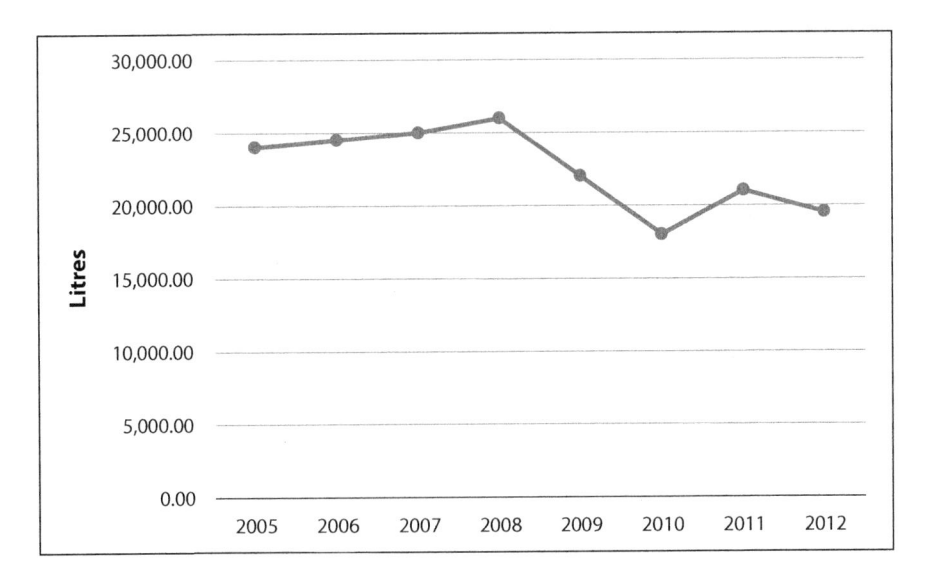

Figure 3.5. Guyana's rum production (thousands of litres)

Source: Bank of Guyana, annual reports.

The Rum Industry of Guyana in the Global Value Chain   77

rums are produced, bulk rum constitutes the largest segment of production and exports.

The industry's major export markets are in Europe and North America (see figure 3.6). Exports to European markets have been roughly twice that of North American markets and stood at US$14 million in 2012.

When exports to the European Union are disaggregated by bulk and bottled, bottled rum exports are miniscule in comparison to bulk rum exports but

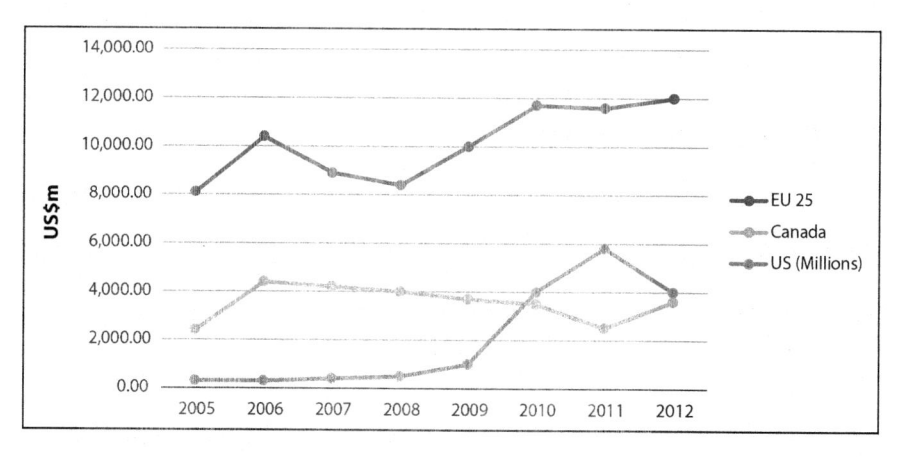

Figure 3.6. Guyana's rum exports by major destinations (US$ millions)
Source: UN COMTRADE database.

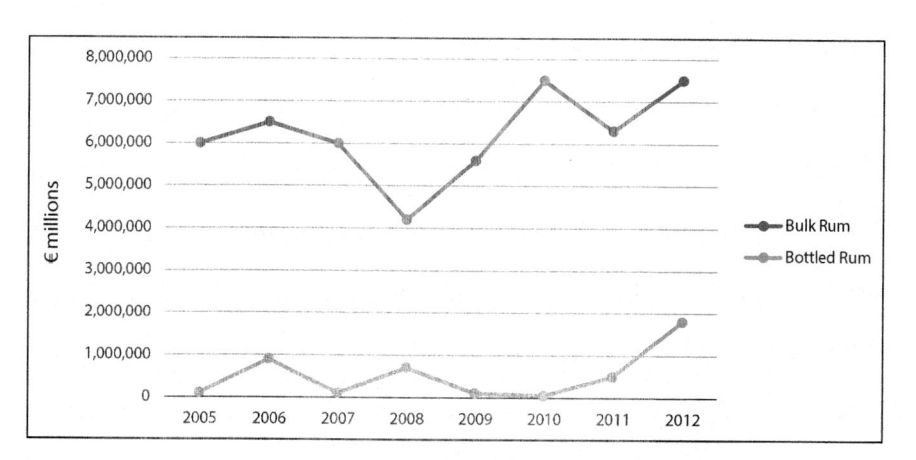

Figure 3.7. Guyana's exports of bulk and bottled rum to the EU25
Source: Eurostat COMEXT database.

displayed upward growth trends between 2010 and 2012. Figure 3.7 shows that while the lesser value-added bulk rum accounts for the greater share of Guyana's rum export to EU markets, the growth rate of value-added rum has been on an upward trajectory. This is likely the result of DDL successfully carving out a niche for itself through the export of twenty-five-year-old dark aged rums.

3.12 Analysis of Factors Affecting Guyana's Competitiveness

Whether sustaining exports of bulk rum or growing a range of premium products, success in the rum industry is achieved through strategies and investments pursued at the firm and industry level. This section summarizes key firm, industry and national factors that explain the relative competitiveness of the rum industry's sustained exports compared to other manufacturing industries in Guyana. This examination also identifies deficits within the industry which, once removed, will greatly enhance the competitiveness of exporting firms on the world market.

3.12.1 Productive Capacity

Both DDL and Banks DIH have ISO-certified quality management systems. Global standards and certification are necessary components of a global competitiveness strategy, especially since rum is a consumer consumable commodity.[2] Rum manufacturing is also capital intensive (Hunte 2012) and requires the hiring and retaining of specialized human capital. Human capital is important in keeping firms at the forefront of both product and process innovations. Both firms have sought to develop their human capital base in-house through scholarship and graduate management trainee programmes. Under the scholarship programmes, students are selected to pursue studies at the state-owned University of Guyana in the areas of engineering, chemistry, management, economics, accounting and marketing. As a condition of scholarship, students are required to enter into a bond of five years of paid service with the provider. In this way, the firms exercise a large measure of control over the availability of their human capital requirements. Since the University of Guyana shares these costs with the state-owned Institute of Applied Science and Technology, the two firms have an advantage in that they do not bear the full cost of educational investment in their innovations.

3.12.2 Infrastructure and Services

The availability and access to quality infrastructure and cheap and reliable supplies of services such as energy, water, transport and information communication technologies are fundamental to the competitiveness of firms in GVCs (OTF Group 2005).

DDL and Banks DIH are energy self-sufficient firms. By utilizing waste for energy generation, their unit cost for energy is far lower than it would be if purchased from the largely fuel-based national grid that has some of the highest energy prices in the world (Kammen and Shirley 2011). As a result, neither firm's production is hindered by high oil prices. Self-sufficiency also extends to water supply. Both firms are producers of potable water on a commercial scale, which is sourced from their respective wells. By being water self-sufficient, both companies have greater control over the quality of their rum production than they would if depending on the unreliable state-owned Guyana Water Incorporated.

Location is also a factor in the industry's competitiveness. By situating production on the eastern bank of the Demerara River, DDL and Banks DIH are in close proximity to Guyana's primary seaports and customs facilities. Their strategic production locations serve as a way of minimizing the cost of global distribution. However, the depth of the Demerara River cannot accommodate large ships, and this increases the cost of imported inputs. In addition, exports from Guyana have to rely on small ships that travel to and from Trinidad and Tobago.

3.12.3 Business Environment

Macroeconomic stability, public governance and access to finance are essential components of a business environment that is conducive to global competitiveness (World Bank 2007). To promote macroeconomic stability, inflation and exchange rates are kept relatively stable in Guyana. The Commercial Court, which was established in 2006, has been instrumental in boosting investor confidence and competitiveness through its timely resolution of commercial disputes

(Government of Guyana 2011) and the modernization of the deeds registry has helped to improve transaction efficiency. The liberalization of the financial sector has led to the establishment of several privately owned commercial banks, two of which are owned by the two leading rum-producing firms. As a result, both companies were well positioned to meet the pre-financing condition for accessing the cost-sharing grant scheme element of the European Union's €70 million Integrated Development Programme for the Caribbean Rum Sector. This four-year programme, which began in August 2002, provided vital financial resources to help the Caribbean rum industry enhance export competitiveness, value addition (bottling and branding), marketing and upgrading of environmental and waste management standards.

3.12.4 Trade and Investment Policy

Guyana's rum exports first gained duty-free access to markets in the European Union and the United States with two trade deals – the Lomé I agreement in 1975 and the Caribbean Basin Economic Recovery Act in 1988. As a result of those trade deals, DDL and Banks DIH have had a presence in markets in the United States and the European Union for more than two and three decades, respectively.

In support of Guyana's access to global markets, the government introduced an automated total revenue integrated processing system, which captured not only revenue collection, but also the streamlining of processes within the trade and customs administration. In light of remaining challenges, it also drafted legislation to support the single window automated processing system, which, once in place, could be accessed online or on site and could halve the processing times for trade transactions.

3.12.5 Institutionalization

DDL and Banks DIH both have a long history in Guyana and their legacy of implementing public-private partnerships can be traced to the seventeenth century. In more recent times, the Public-Private Dialogue Body – which was established under the National Competitiveness Strategy – has reviewed shortcomings and made recommendations on actions to be taken to streamline import-export processes and procedures.

3.13 Role of Key Stakeholders in Guyana's Rum Industry

Table 3.7 summarizes the main roles, level of importance and influence of the primary and secondary stakeholders in Guyana's rum industry. The primary stakeholders are the state-owned Guyana Sugar Corporation and the University of Guyana, the privately owned Guyana Telephone and Telegraph Company, Digicel, Citizens and Demerara banks, and WIRSPA. Each stakeholder plays a very important role in the industry and shapes its development by wielding significant power and influence.

The secondary stakeholders, on the other hand, include governmental ministries, semi-autonomous agencies, institutions and industry associations. Most play an indirect role in Guyana's rum industry. However, their general functions have the ability to influence the industry's development.

3.14 Upgrading Strategies and Tactics

Upgrading enables firms to improve their competitiveness. Both DDL and Banks DIH has been able to remain competitive and sustain exports as a result of several upgrading strategies and tactics. Under the GVC framework, firms can pursue four types of upgrading strategies: (1) product upgrading, (2) process upgrading, (3) functional upgrading and (4) chain or inter-sectoral upgrading (Gereffi and Fernandez-Stark 2011). Table 3.8 summarizes the upgrading trajectories and respective undertakings of Guyana's two main rum producers over the years.

Improvements to the product were achieved by introducing premium lines of DDL rum under the El Dorado brand of rums in 1992. Additionally, the company re-entered the low alcoholic market in 2012 with the reintroduction of Five-O, a vodka cooler and a cranberry-flavoured vodka under the Ivanoff brand.

Improvements to the manufacturing process were achieved through investment in capital-intensive equipment to enhance automation. In 2013, DDL committed US$7 million towards upgrading its power-generation facility, production equipment and fleet and storage facilities.

Both companies have sought to upgrade market access. For instance, Banks DIH launched its XM line of rum in Europe after successfully introducing it to the Caribbean market. DDL has accessed those markets through the establishment of subsidiaries in India, the United States and the Netherlands.

Table 3.7. Key Stakeholders in the Guyana Rum Industry

Primary Stakeholders	Main Role/Principal Interest	Level of Importance in the Industry	Power to Influence Change in the Industry
GuySuCo	Supplier of molasses	High	Medium
University of Guyana	Human capital development	High	High
GT&T and Digicel	ICT	High	Medium
Commercial banks (Citizens and Demerara banks)	Investment financing	High	High
West Indies Rum and Spirits Association	Promote the development of Caribbean rum as a premium category	High	High

Secondary Stakeholders	Main Role/Principal Interest	Level of Importance in the Industry	Power to Influence Change in the Industry
Ministry of Foreign Trade	Negotiating and securing favourable trade policies	High	High
Ministry of Finance	Macroeconomic stability	High	High
Ministry of Transport and Hydraulics	Transport infrastructure – air, land, and sea.	High	High

Institution	Role		
Bank of Guyana	Exchange rate policies	High	High
Environmental Protection Agency	Enforcing compliance with environmental regulations	High	High
Guyana Revenue Authority	Taxation and customs administration	High	High
Guyana Office for Investment	Trade and investment facilitation	High	High
National Bureau of Standards	Enforce quality and standards compliance	High	High
National Competitiveness Council	Oversees the implementation of the national competitiveness strategy	High	High
Public-Private Dialogue Body	Reviews shortcomings and makes recommendations on actions to be taken to streamline import-export processes and procedures	High	High
Guyana Manufacturers and Services Association	Supports manufacturing in Guyana through technical assistance and policy advocacy	High	Medium
Georgetown Chamber of Commerce and Industry	Promoting and protecting the interests of members through policy advocacy	High	Low
Private Sector Commission	Policy advocacy	Medium	Medium

Table 3.8. Guyana's Rum Industry Upgrading Strategies

Strategy	Undertakings
Product upgrading	DDL began manufacturing and exporting older aged rums in the El Dorado range of Demerara rums.
Process upgrading	Installation of capital-intensive equipment to increase automation of the rum manufacturing facilities.
Functional upgrading	Establishment and marketing "Authentic Caribbean Rum" as an umbrella brand that allows Caribbean rum producers to differentiate their products at a lower cost to each producer.
End market upgrading	Banks DIH launched its XM family of rums – previously sold regionally in the EU market. Establishment of subsidiaries and formation of associations in key export markets.

Table 3.9. Upgrading Tactics of the Firms in Guyana's Rum Industry

Tactics	Undertakings
Human capital development (product, process, and functional upgrading)	Provision of scholarships for training in science and technology at the University of Guyana.
Access to finance (product, process, and functional upgrading)	Establishment of industry-based commercial banks for investment financing. Lobbied the European Union for transitional financing (integrated development programme for the Caribbean rum sector) in response to changes in its trade policy.
Access to markets (end market upgrading)	Participation in several international competitions for spirits (the International Wine and Spirit Competition, London; the International Rum Festival, Canada; the International Spirits Challenge, London; and the Spirit Business Rum Masters Awards, London) Raise awareness on quality and reliability of supply Make direct contact with buyers and explore market opportunities.

Table 3.9 condenses the tactics undertaken by DDL and Banks DIH. Some of the initiatives pursued by these firms have been facilitated by the European Union's Integrated Development Programme for the Caribbean Rum Sector, previously mentioned.

3.15 SWOT Analysis of Guyana's Rum Industry

Table 3.10 summarizes the strengths, weaknesses, threats and opportunities of Guyana's rum industry. DDL and Banks DIH's experience, including access to raw materials, physical capital, among other factors, shows that successful upgrading in the global market is feasible.

Although firms have been doing their part internally to enhance competitiveness, challenges remain at the national level. Noteworthy is the political environment surrounding the publicly owned sugar industry which has been plagued by both structural and governance-related problems, resulting in the decline of sugar production (Thomas 2012). This may threaten the competitive advantage of DDL, which is the sole consumer of molasses produced by the sugar company. This must be considered within the context of competing multinational firms that are undertaking investments and contract arrangements along the value chain to secure supplies of inputs.

The industry's largest segment is bulk rum purchased by leading rum companies in Europe and the United States. A key consideration for surviving in this market is the ability of firms to compete on the basis of price (given the relative lack of economies of scale) with rum manufacturers from other regions perceived to be low-cost producers, such as countries in Central and South America that are supplying some of the same bulk purchasers of DDL and Banks DIH's rums. According to Laurent (n.d.), while "Caribbean brands have been enjoying successes on the quality front ... price competitiveness is still the major determining factor for the bulk of rum sales on the international market".

Table 3.10. SWOT Analysis of Guyana's Rum Industry

Strengths	Weaknesses	Opportunities	Threats
• Experience • Leadership • Physical capital (plant and equipment) • Quality certification • Access to skilled human resources • Access to raw materials	• State of domestic sugar industry • Small size of the industry • Lack of economies of scale for bulk rum production • Shipping infrastructure	• Growth in key segment globally, including dark, aged, flavoured and white rums. • Use diaspora to expand presence in markets, such as Canada and the United States.	• US subsidies • Unsustainability of the domestic sugar industry • Preference erosion

Even though firms face stiff competition from leading brands in the markets in which they operate, DDL has a niche in dark aged rums. In fact, due to its consistent quality and flavours (Dykstra 2013), Guyana is known for its Demerara rums (www.tastings.com). In addition to awards at the International Wine and Spirits Competition for the El Dorado brand of rums, DDL's El Dorado fifteen-year reserve is mentioned as one of the fifty best rums in the world (http://www.thefiftybest.com/spirits/best_rum/4/). These accomplishments are indications of one new direction for the industry – increased production of quality, dark aged rums.

This potential is reinforced by the fact that there is international growth in the aged and dark rums segments (Drinks Trade 2010, 2014; WIRSPA 2013a). Dark rums dominate in the global rum industry, accounting for 61 per cent of global market share (Top 5 of Anything 2014). A successful producer of high-value products, DDL can secure its competitive strength in the export of dark aged rums by ramping up branding and upscaling strategies that Pernod Ricard has successfully utilized in the past. Furthermore, DDL and Banks DIH can look to create subsidiary and collaborative arrangements in markets where they currently do not have a strong presence, notably the United States. These are strategies that Banks DIH can certainly emulate to enhance its competitive strength and export of white rums under the XM label.

Given Guyana's agricultural potential, the industry can also exploit factors not fully tapped into at present, such as creating fruit-flavoured rums. DDL is already heading in this direction with its recent launch of cranberry-flavoured vodka. White rums and flavoured rum segments are also displaying positive growth trends (Drinks Trade 2010, 2014; WIRSPA 2013a).

3.16 Lessons Learned

The following points summarize the lessons learned from the study of Guyana's participation in the rum GVC:

- The global rum industry is dominated by a few large multinationals in developed countries (where the bulk of the value added takes place), removed from where rum is actually produced in developing countries.
- Vertical integration in the rum industry is necessary to control final quality characteristics that are crucial for brand recognition and successful marketing.

- The local rum industry in Guyana reflects many of the success factors in the global rum industry, inclusive of dominance by a few large companies and vertical integration of operations.
- Guyana exports most of its rum as bulk rum for blending, bottling and branding by global lead firms.
- DDL has carved a niche for itself through the export of dark aged rums as old as twenty-five years, which are regarded as premium spirits.
- The regional industry association (WIRSPA) has been effective in helping to enhance the marketing of Guyanese rum on the basis of quality and authenticity.
- The major consuming markets for rum are in Europe and the United States, with Germany and Spain being both the global leader in exports and imports of rum.
- Demand growth in emerging markets is trending upwards.

3.17 Recommendations for Further Upgrading

3.17.1 Recommendations for Product Upgrading

- DDL should seek to increase the production and exportation of bottled rum as this is the higher-value segment of the market.
- DDL should use its established reputation in the premium rum market to introduce greater product differentiation through "exotic Caribbean" fruit-flavoured rums. Banks DIH can similarly consider product differentiation through fruit-flavoured rums.

3.17.2 Recommendations for Process Upgrading

- Firms can establish backward linkages by establishing contract arrangements with farmers for the possible range of fruits which can be used in product expansion.
- Support farmers to engage in best farming practices through financing, technical assistance, purchase guarantees and so on.
- Undertake greater investment in research and development and/or establishment of strategic links with the University of Guyana, the

Caribbean Agricultural Research and Development Institute and other such institutions to support the process of new product development.

3.17.3 Recommendations for Functional Upgrading

- DDL and Banks DIH should seek to exploit greater export market penetration by fully utilizing the established "authentic" labelling developed by WIRSPA.
- Partially privatizing the state-owned monopoly sugar industry to ensure consistent and cost-effective supply of molasses domestically. Rum producers can be given the opportunity to hold shares in the company and have a stake in its development.

3.17.4 Recommendations for End Market Upgrading

- Seek to penetrate emerging markets such as in Asia and South America through the establishment of subsidiaries, acquisition of indigenous firms in these markets, or other partnership arrangements.
- Seek further penetration into Europe's two largest consumer markets for rum – Germany and Spain.

3.18 Policy Recommendations

The following policy measures would greatly enhance the value creation of the rum industry:

- Increasing public investment in tertiary-level institutions to increase the quality of the skills of the labour pool available to rum manufacturers.
- Creation of a deep-water harbour to improve shipping facilities available to manufacturers and increase capacity for shipments into and out of Guyana. This could offer substantial benefits for the global competitiveness of the industry.
- Collaboration with the Ministry of Foreign Trade and the Caribbean Community secretariat on policy advocacy. Removal of United States subsidies on US-related manufacturers should be a priority in this regard.

- Adopting a national system of innovation that can serve as a model for sharing the cost and risks associated with this survival tool (Cavusgil, Calantone and Zhao 2003).

3.19 Conclusion

Using the GVC framework, this case study examined the factors responsible for Guyana's sustained competitiveness in the global rum industry. The local sector, which has a duopolistic structure, has been able to successfully operate at the "rum production" stage of the GVC where significant value is created. This is evident by consistent exports and quality recognition on the international market. The factors responsible for the country's success range from its natural resources and favourable climatic conditions to the prudent business strategies of its leading firms. Given the challenges faced by the industry, particularly in the bulk rum segment, the most probable strategy for cementing and expanding the presence of the country in the global GVC is the production of branded aged, dark, white and fruit-flavoured rums supported by subsidiaries and the formation of business alliances to secure market access in favourable markets where the country's presence is weak.

Notes

1. The pre-eminence of the Caribbean as a producing region is reflected by the fact that in the United States, distilleries market their rums using Caribbean-themed names. See http://www.tastings.com/spirits/rum.html.
2. For this reason, WIRSPA encourages its members to follow strict international regulations.

References

Bacardi. 2013. Annual Report. Hamilton, Bermuda: Bacardi.
Banks DIH Ltd. 2012. Annual Report. Georgetown: Banks DIH Ltd.
———.n.d. Accessed March 2014. http://www.banksdih.com/?q=abour-us/history; http://www.specialitybrands.com/press/xm/xm-vxo_rum.pdf.
Barceló. 2014. Annual Report. https://www.barcelo.com/BarceloHotels/.../barcelo_memoria_2014_completa_en21-1.

BBC News. 2012. "Diageo Buys Majority Stake in India's United Spirits". London, 9 November. http://www.bbc.com/news/business-20267619.

Cooper, B. 2009. "Rum No Longer Just a Consolation Prize". 6 February. http://www.just-drinks.com/analysis/report-in-focus-rum-no-longer-just-a-consolation-prize_id96241.aspx.

Cavusgil, S., R. Calantone and Y. Zhao. 2003. "Tacit Knowledge Transfer and Firm Innovation Capability". *Journal of Business and Industrial Marketing* 18 (1): 6–21.

CIA (Central Intelligence Agency). 2014. *World Fact Book*. Accessed 22 June. https://www.cia.gov/library/publications/the-world-factbook/geos/gy.html.

DDL (Demerara Distillers Limited). 2012. Annual Report. Georgetown, Guyana.

Diageo. 2014. Annual Report 2013/2014. London, England.

———. N.d. *Diageo Latin America and Caribbean.* http://www.diageo.com/en-us/ourbusiness/ourregions/Pages/Diageo-Latin-America-and-Caribbean.aspx.

Drinks Trade. 2010. "Moving Beyond Mojito". http://www.drinkstrade.com.au/ContentFiles/Documents/Drinks%20Trade/Public/Library/features/spirits/Issues%2016%20Apr-May%2010%20Moving%20beyond%20Mojito%20-20Light%20and%20dark%20rums%20feastures.pdf.

———. 2014. *International Wine and Spirits Record: Global Liquor Trends.* http://www.drinkstrade.com.au/ContentFiles/Documents/Drinks%20Trade/Public/Library/profiles/wine/Issue%2004%20Apr-May%2008%20Global%20Liquor%20Trends%20International%20Wine%20and%20Spirits%20Record%20Agata%20Andrzejczak%20profiles.pdf.

Dykstra, C. 2013. "El Dorado 3 Year Cask Aged Demerara Rum". *Rum Howler.* http://therumhowlerblog.wordpress.com/rum-reviews/white-rums/el-dorado-3-year-cask-aged-demerara-rum/.

Gereffi, G., and K. Fernandez-Stark. 2011. *Global Value Chain Analysis: A Primer.* Durham, NC: Duke University Center on Globalization, Governance and Competitiveness. http://www.cggc.duke.edu/pdfs/2011-05-31_GVC_analysis_a_primer.pdf.

Government of Guyana. 2011. *National Competitiveness Stategy Evaluation Report.* Georgetown: Government of Guyana. http://www.competitiveness.org.gy/ncs_final report.pdf.

Hunte, K. 2012. "The Importance of Trade Adjustment Support to the Caribbean Rum Industry". *Estey Centre Journal of International Law and Trade Policy* 13 (1): 43–55.

ITC (International Trade Centre). n.d. Trade Map. http://www.trademap.org/

Just Drinks. 2009. "International Rum: Forecasts to 2012". www.just-drinks.com/store/…/2009_aroq_international_rum_sample.pdf.

———. 2013. "Global Market Review of Rum: Forecasts to 2017". http://www.just-drinks.com/market-research/global-market-review-of-rum-forecasts-to-2017_id167193.aspx.

Kammen, D., and R. Shirley. 2011. "Renewable Energy Sector Development in the Caribbean: Current Trends and Lessons from History". http://rael.berkeley.edu/sites/default/files/Kammen-Shirley-JEPO.pdf.

Laurent, E. N.d. "Turbulent Times for Rum: EU Preferences". *Caribbean Intelligence*. http://www.caribbeanintelligenceu/com/content/turbulent-times-rum-eu-preferences.

OTF Group. 2005. "Improving Competitiveness and Increasing Economic Growth in Tanzania: The Role of Information and Communication Technologies". Information for Development Program, Washington, DC. http://www.infodev.org/infordev-files/resource/InfodevDocuments_81.pdf.

Pardis Cognac. 2014. "Bacardi Launched D'usse XO at $275 in 11 States in the USA". 8 June. https://cognacs.wordpress.com/2014/06/08/bacardi-launched-dusse-xo-at-275-in-11-states-in-the-usa/.

Pernod Ricard. 2013. Annual Report 2012/2013. Paris, France.

Tanduay Holdings. 2013. Annual Report. http://www.pds.com.ph/wp-content/uploads/2014/04/Disclosure-No-417-2014-annual-Report-for-Fiscal-Year-Ended-December-31-2013-SEC-FORM-17-A.pdf.

Thomas, C.Y. 2012. "Guyana Economic Performance and Outlook (The Recent Scramble for Natural Resources)". Georgetown, Guyana. http://idsguyana.org/articles/professor-clive-thomas/new-menu/11-guyana-economic-performance-and-outlook-the-recent-scramble-for-natural-resources.html.

Top 5 of Anything. 2014. "The Top 5 Best Selling Brands of Rum Worldwide". http://top5ofanything.com/index.php?h=a515a8c9.

United Spirits. 2014. Annual Report 2013–2014. Bangalore, India.

———. n.d. About us. http://unitedspirits.in/aboutus.aspx.

WIRSPA (West Indies Rum and Spirits Association). 2013a. "Decade of Rum". www.harpers.co.uk/download.

———. 2013b. "Rum Making". http://www.wirspa.com/rum-making.html.

Whiskey Exchange. 2014. "Newfoundland Screech Rum". https://www.thewhiskeyexchange.com/P-21980.aspx.

Winchester Capital Research. 2014. "Mergers and Acquisitions Global Insight: The Spirits Industry in 2014". http://winchestercapital.com/wp-content/uploads/2014/09/Winchester-Research-Spirits-Indsutry-Review.pdf.

World Bank. 2007. *Guyana: Investment Climate Assessment,* volume 1, *Main Findings and Policy Recommendations*. Washington, DC: World Bank. https://openknowledge.worldbank.org/handle/10986/7865.

CASE STUDY 4

VincyFresh Limited
A Caribbean Case Study on Export Competitiveness and Global Value Chain Analysis

HEIDI E. VINCENT
Owner and Lead Consultant
Quality Solutions for Business Excellence, Grenada

SIMONE N. MURRAY
Managing Director
Business Logistics Incorporated

Abstract

This case study will focus on VincyFresh Limited, an exporting agro-processing company located on the Eastern Caribbean island of St Vincent and the Grenadines. Although it is not a best-practice case, it assesses a firm that faces many of the common competitiveness issues encountered by Caribbean companies. The report uses the global value chain (GVC) framework for its study and focuses on a seven-year period from 2008 to 2012. It examines domestic, regional and international market conditions along with lead firms and exporters or importers in the sector. Particular attention is given to five key factors that typically affect developing countries' competitiveness in GVCs: productive capacity, infrastructure and services, business environment, trade and investment policy, and institutionalization.

Finally, we use the VincyFresh journey towards becoming an exporter, its challenges along the way and how it fits into the fruit and vegetable GVC to derive recommendations, both for the development of the company and to provide invaluable learning for other Caribbean businesses aspiring to become fruit and vegetable exporter companies or producer-exporter companies and those struggling to stay relevant in the fruit and vegetable GVC.

4.1 Introduction

The banana market's loss of preferential access to the European Union over the past fifteen years has had a profound effect on the economic development strategies of St Vincent and the Grenadines. In the 1980s and early 1990s, the annual export earnings from the banana industry averaged US$37.5 million; by 2010, earnings had fallen to US$2.35 million (IMF 2011).

Between 1990 and 1999, banana exports from St Vincent and the Grenadines declined by 54 per cent from 81,155 tonnes in 1990 to 37,376 tonnes in 1999 (SVG–EU 2002). The banana sector was also affected by the Black Sigatoka disease[1] which arrived in the Caribbean in 1991 and "has since spread, reportedly reducing the value of exports from St Vincent and the Grenadines by 90%" (BBC 2013).

"The share of agriculture in GDP declined from 21.2 per cent in 1990 to 9.6 per cent in 2006" and continued to contract "in the face of continued uncertainty surrounding the EU banana regime and adverse weather conditions" (SVG–EU 2008).

These changes and challenges highlighted the need for the government to pursue an agricultural diversification strategy. The government has focused on building an industry around the transformation of primary resources into processed value-added products in an effort to boost exports.

This case study focuses on VincyFresh, an agro-processing company that was established as a joint venture between WinFresh (60 per cent) and the government-owned National Properties Limited (40 per cent). The Ministry of Agriculture in St Vincent and the Grenadines has identified VincyFresh as a business that can help diversify the economy. This case study will investigate whether such expectations are realistic. It will do this by examining the company's place in the processing segment of the fruit and vegetables GVC. Later sections will also evaluate VincyFresh's position within the GVC and make recommendations on how the company can improve its position along the value chain.

4.2 The Global Fruit and Vegetable Processing Industry

There are five main segments within the fruit and vegetable GVC: inputs, production, packing and storage, processing and distribution, and marketing (Fernandez-Stark, Bamber and Gereffi 2011). This is illustrated in figure 4.1.

Industry analysts predict that pre-cut frozen vegetables and pre-made sales will be important growth markets moving forward, while trade in fresh fruit and vegetables is also expected to remain robust (Report Linker 2013). Section 4.2.1 explores the lead firms and the top export and import markets in the fruit and vegetable processing industry.[2]

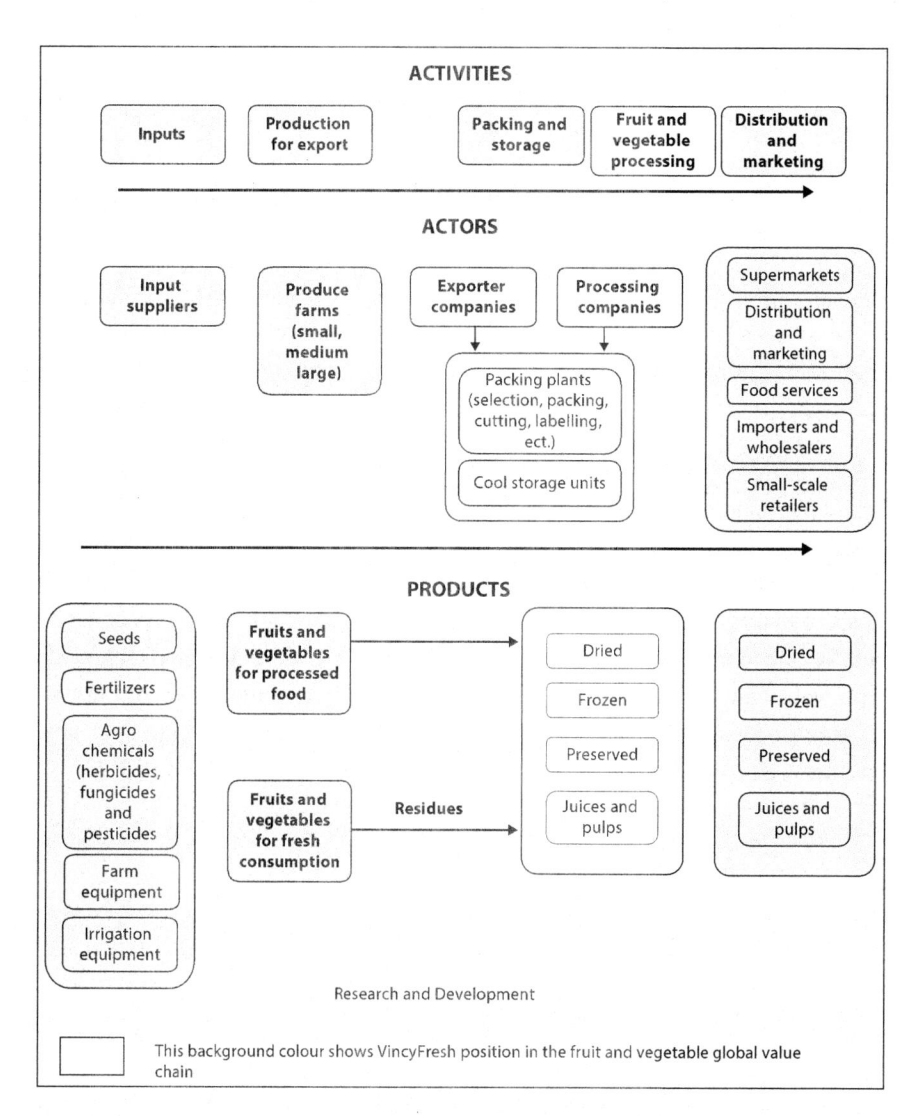

Figure 4.1. VincyFresh within the fruit and vegetable global value chain
Source: Authors' adaptation from Fernandez-Stark, Bamber and Gereffi (2011).

4.2.1 Lead Firms in the Fruit and Vegetable Processing Industry

The key lead firm types in the fruit and vegetable processing industry are mass merchants and brand manufacturers. Mass merchants are department or discount stores such as Walmart, Costco and Target that carry their own private labels;

Table 4.1. Lead Firms in the Fruit and Vegetable Processing Industry

Lead Firm Type	Type of Brand	Description	Examples
Retailers: Mass merchants	Private label	Departmental/discount stores carry private label	Walmart, Asda, Costco, Target and Tesco
Brand manufacturers	National brand	Firms own brand name and manufacturers	Del Monte, Heinz, J.R. Simplot, McCain Foods, Bonduelle, Agrana, Pinguin, La Doria, ConAgra and General Mills

brand manufacturers are companies that have their own brand name and manufacturers such as Del Monte, Heinz and others (see table 4.1). These lead firms generally acquire raw materials from contract growers who grow specific varieties of plants according to processor requirements. Supply contracts generally run for one to ten years. Long-term contracts are generally negotiated by growers who would have to plant to fulfil the need of certain manufacturers but not see returns for several years. When growers and manufacturers enter into long-term contracts, price is often negotiated on an annual basis (First Research 2013).

4.2.2 Lead Exporters and Importers

The top five global exporters and importers in 2010 for each of the product classifications in which VincyFresh exports are examined in table 4.2.

Specific opportunities for export exist in the following areas, where the import share of each country is significantly higher than its export share:

- Fruit juices: United States (exports 8 per cent; imports 13 per cent)
- Fruit juices: Germany (exports 7 per cent; imports 11 per cent)
- Fruit juices: Netherlands (exports 8 per cent; imports 12 per cent)
- Roots and tubers: China (exports 12 per cent; imports 44 per cent)

It should also be noted that in the case of sauces and seasonings, jams and jellies – some of the lead importers, such as the United Kingdom, the United States, Germany and France are also lead exporters in similar or greater quantity.

Table 4.2. Lead Exporters and Importers in the Fruit and Vegetable Processing Industry

Sauces and Seasonings

	Lead Exporters			Lead Importers		
	Country	%	$ Share (m)	Country	%	$ Share (m)
2010 total value	1. United States	13.0	$1,100.0	1. United Kingdom	10.0	$780.0
Export: $8,701,886,761	2. Netherlands	9.6	$790.0	2. United States	9.8	$770.0
Import: $8,165,609,643	3. Germany	8.1	$670.0	3. France	7.1	$560.0
	4. Italy	6.9	$570.0	4. Germany	6.1	$470.0
	5. China	6.0	$490.0	5. Canada	5.8	$450.0
	Total	**43.6**	**$3,620.0**	**Total**	**38.8**	**$3,030.0**

Jams and Jellies

	Lead Exporters			Lead Importers		
	Country	%	$ Share (m)	Country	%	$ Share (m)
2010 total value	1. France	14.0	$290.0	1. Germany	10.0	$200.0
Export: $2,188,937,849	2. Germany	10.0	$200.0	2. United States	9.7	$180.0
Import: $1,981,385,489	3. Italy	5.9	$120.0	3. France	9.4	$180.0
	4. Chile	5.3	$110.0	4. Netherlands	6.2	$120.0
	5. Turkey	5.0	$100.0	5. United Kingdom	6.2	$120.0
	Total	**40.2**	**$820.0**	**Total**	**41.5**	**$800.0**

Fruit Juices

	Lead Exporters			Lead Importers		
	Country	%	$ Share (m)	Country	%	$ Share (m)
2010 total value	1. Brazil	19.0	$2,300.0	1. United States	13.0	$1,500.0
Export: $13,305,381,519	2. United States	8.4	$1,000.0	2. Netherlands	12.0	$1,400.0
Import: $12,692,503,599	3. Netherlands	7.8	$970.0	3. Germany	11.0	$1,300.0
	4. Germany	7.3	$900.0	4. France	8.7	$1,000.0
	5. China	6.8	$840.0	5. United Kingdom	7.6	$860.0
	Total	**49.3**	**$6,010.0**	**Total**	**52.3**	**$6,060.0**

(*Table 4.2 continues*)

Table 4.2. Lead Exporters and Importers in the Fruit and Vegetable Processing Industry (continued)

Frozen Fruits and Nuts	Lead Exporters			Lead Importers		
	Country	%	$ Share (m)	Country	%	$ Share (m)
2010 total value	1. Poland	15.0	$430.0	1. Germany	18.0	$490.0
Export: $2,994,109,934	2. China	9.0	$260.0	2. United States	15.0	$410.0
Import: $2,821,281,875	3. Serbia	8.8	$250.0	3. France	11.0	$280.0
	4. Chile	8.1	$230.0	4. Netherlands	7.4	$200.0
	5. Canada	7.5	$210.0	5. Canada	4.4	$120.0
	Total	48.4	$1,380.0	Total	55.8	$1,500.0

Fresh and Dried Vegetables, Roots and Tubers	Lead Exporters			Lead Importers		
	Country	%	$ Share (m)	Country	%	$ Share (m)
2010 total value	1. Thailand	35.0	$920.0	1. China	44.0	$1,100.0
Export: $2,587,303,468	2. China	12.0	$310.0	2. Japan	6.4	$170.0
Import: $2,587,303,468	3. Vietnam	8.2	$210.0	3. United States	8.1	$210.0
	4. Germany	5.7	$150.0	4. Germany	5.1	$130.0
	5. United States	5.5	$140.0	5. United Kingdom	3.6	$94.0
	Total	66.4	$1,730.0	Total	67.2	$1,704.0

4.3 VincyFresh in the Fruit and Vegetable Global Value Chain

VincyFresh, the focus of this case study, is an agro-processing firm based in Kingstown, St Vincent and the Grenadines.

Of the five main segments within the fruit and vegetable GVC – inputs, production, packing and storage, processing, and distribution and marketing (Fernandez-Stark, Bamber and Gereffi 2011) – VincyFresh is currently involved in only two of those segments – packing and storage, and processing (see figure 4.1).

VincyFresh receives inputs for both segments from joint venture partner National Properties Limited and other small farmers on a contractual basis. Seedlings are provided to contracted farmers through the Ministry of Agriculture via the Taiwanese Technical Mission and through the government nursery at Dumbarton.

The various fruits and vegetables, obtained year-round, are packaged as either fresh produce or dried, frozen, preserved or processed into juices and pulps for use in a range of products. The company has a total of seven product lines under the brand name "Winfresh": sauces, seasonings and marinades, jellies and jams, syrups and cordials, herbs and spices, frozen fruit, and fresh produce (see table 4.3).

In the packing and storage segment of the value chain, VincyFresh selects, packages and labels fresh fruits and vegetables before exporting the products to its 100 per cent subsidiary WinFresh UK Limited based in the United Kingdom, and Caribbean Fruit Connections, a fresh fruit and vegetable merchant

Table 4.3. VincyFresh Product Lines and Ranges

Product Line	Product Range	Product Line	Product Range
Sauces	Pepper, sweet chili, honey and garlic chili sauces	Herbs and spices	Basil, celery, ginger parsley, hot pepper
Seasonings and marinades	Green seasoning and herb, garlic and ginger, herb and pepper marinades	Frozen fruit	Frozen mango, guava, papaya, golden apple, grapefruit, orange, sible sweet, lime lemon pulp
Jellies and jams	Pepper, mango-pepper, ginger-pepper jellies		
Syrups and cordials	Ginger syrup, sorrel and lime cordials	Fresh produce	Dasheen, roasted breadfruit, callaloo

wholesaler located in Miami, Florida, United States. Although its association with Caribbean Fruit Connections proves convenient, VincyFresh should explore varied and/or more profitable distribution and marketing options in the United States.

VincyFresh mainly exports its processed products within the regional market to other Caribbean islands, namely Antigua, Trinidad and Tobago, Barbados, Grenada, and Dominica (see table 4.4). The company began exporting in 2010, just three years after it was established. In that first year, it earned 78.5 per cent of its total earnings (US$87,860) from dasheen[3] and golden apple exports to the United Kingdom. By 2012, the company's export earnings had more than doubled to US$203,166, and one year later, exports accounted for more than 75 per cent of VincyFresh's total revenue. The remaining 20–25 per cent comes from processed fruit and vegetable sales to five main local supermarkets: CFL SVG Limited, C.K. Greave and Company Limited, Knights Trading Limited, Canouan Food Stores, and L.A. Grocery.

Despite its increasing revenue position over the reported four-year period from 2010 to 2014, VincyFresh has experienced continued fluctuating losses. There was a loss of US$381,501 in 2010 when the company began exporting, which increased to US$657,505 in 2012 and then declined considerably to US$370,190 in 2014. VincyFresh has cited four main interrelated reasons for its continuous losses:

1. difficulty in accessing additional finance for equipment purchase, other capital investments, training and standards implementation;
2. insufficiently trained workers;
3. non-functional plant equipment and plant equipment that needs to be upgraded; and
4. underutilized plant capacity: VincyFresh currently only utilizes about 30–40 per cent of its plant capacity.

VincyFresh has also begun working towards becoming Hazard Analysis and Critical Control Points certified in order to support its access to markets in most of its targeted territories. However, this takes time to implement and is costly to achieve and maintain.

Although the company more than tripled its staff in the first five years of operation, its workforce is relatively small, with seventeen employees in 2013 (see appendix 4.1). Five of the workers attended college or university. In terms of staff development, VincyFresh engages in a mix of internal and external

Table 4.4. VincyFresh Export Statistics

Export products	2010	2012	2014
	Dasheen: 4,453 boxes Golden apples: 1,130 boxes	Dasheen: 10,517 boxes Assorted products:* 50 cases	Dasheen: 3,868 boxes Pepper mash: 26,167 pounds Fresh hot peppers: 3,430 pounds Assorted products:* 917 cases
Export revenue (EC$)	$237,222.89	$548,549.04	$377,612.51
Export revenue (US$)	$87,860.33	$203,166.31	$139,856.49
Total revenue (EC$)	$302,016.94	$729,022.61	$589,841.78
Total revenue (US$)	$111,858.13	$270,008.37	$218,459.92
Export revenue as a % of total revenue (US$)	78.55%	75.24%	64.02%

	Regional	International
Export markets	Antigua, Trinidad, Barbados, Tortola, Grenada, Dominica	United States, United Kingdom
Export products	Seasonings and marinades, jams and jellies, syrups and cordials, frozen fruit pulps	**Fresh Produce:** Dasheen, hot peppers Golden apples (2010 only)

*Assorted products: Seasonings and marinades, jams and jellies, syrups and cordials, frozen fruit pulps.
Source: VincyFresh Ltd.

training initiatives – in 2012, eight staff members attended external sessions on food handling, hygiene and fire drills.

4.4 The Fruit Vegetable Processing Industry in St Vincent and the Grenadines

The main suppliers for St Vincent and the Grenadines' fruit and vegetable processing industry are farmers and vendors. Farmers serve the supply chain by providing produce to supermarkets, vendors, agro-processors, traders, institutions and the general population.

While the inconsistent supply of produce is one of the challenges facing the fruit and vegetable processing industry, there are also opportunities (see table 4.5), such as the strong demand that exists for niche agricultural products like dasheen (also called taro) and the potential to expand into other regional markets through the CARICOM Single Market and Economy.[4]

In response to the challenge of inconsistent supply of produce, the government has partnered with the Food and Agriculture Organization and the Taiwan International Cooperation and Development Fund to establish a framework for development assistance.

Between January 2011 and December 2013, the Government of St Vincent and the Grenadines engaged in a technical cooperation programme with the Taiwan International Cooperation and Development Fund, valued at US$1,535,000 with the following key objectives (ICDF 2013):

1. Train farmers to build the capacity to cultivate local alternatives to imported vegetables during rainy seasons through greenhouse-based production.
2. Establish a supply chain for vegetable seedlings and a wholesale marketing chain.
3. Improve facilities and production technologies associated with the development of alternative crops such as tomato, sweet pepper and cucumber.
4. Establish seedling production facilities.
5. Establish production and marketing groups by region (for example, greenhouse groups) and crop characteristics (for example, pineapple and watermelon groups).
6. Assist and provide guidance to farmers to organize production and marketing groups so as to improve cultivation techniques and marketing abilities, producing 375 tons of agricultural produce.

In December 2013, torrential rains and high winds resulted in overflowing rivers and flash flooding which dealt severe damage to both St Vincent's and St Lucia's agriculture sectors.

The Food and Agriculture Organization "formally signed livelihood rehabilitation and resilience building assistance totaling US$630,000" for both St Lucia and St Vincent and the Grenadines. St Vincent's agricultural sector, which was considered the harder hit by the disaster, received "US$320,000 to quickly rehabilitate the affected farmers" (*Jamaica Observer*, 4 March 2014).

Table 4.5. SWOT Analysis of the Agro-Processing Industry in St Vincent and the Grenadines

Strengths	Weaknesses
• Fertile volcanic soil • Relative short distances to regional and US markets • Good supply of water for irrigation • Availability of a range of exotic tropical fruits and vegetables • Market access through non-reciprocal preferential agreements with selected industrialized nations	• An inconsistent and insufficient supply of raw material • Limited farmable lands (hilly topography) • High losses during transport from farm to factory • Inappropriate or obsolete processing and ancillary equipment • Inconsistent product quality • Suboptimal use of processing facilities and equipment • Poorly trained personnel • Inappropriate packaging materials and high packaging cost • Weak institutional support for non-banana crops • Marketing of agricultural crops is very weak • Weak or non-existent market development • Scarcity of financing and the low level of entrepreneurship and management training • Antiquated farming methods • Poor harvesting practices • Poor feeder road maintenance

(*Table 4.5. continues*)

Table 4.5. SWOT Analysis of the Agro-Processing Industry in St Vincent and the Grenadines (*continued*)

Opportunities	Threats
• Strong demand for agricultural products (niche markets) • Access to financial resources (European Union, Caribbean Development Bank, local government) • Linkages with tourism, agro-processors and other stake-holders along the agro-processing food chain • Rural development and poverty alleviation • Product development and market differentiation • Conservation and environmental enhancement • Globalization and trade liberalization of World Trade Organization rules and agreements • Expanding market through the Caribbean Single Market and Economy • Increasing demand for safe and good quality products • Growing tourism industry (hotel food supply)	• Vulnerability of sector to natural hazards (hurricanes, volcanic eruption) • Decline in global market prices for agro-products can negatively impact the sustainability of the industry • Environmental degradation • Absence of a land utilization policy • Competition from foreign large-scale producers • Non-tariff barriers in target markets • Ageing farming population and seeming lack of interest in farm labour

Source: Adapted from the Government of St Vincent and the Grenadines' National Export Strategy, 2009.

In order to assist local farmers with mitigating the ever-present threat of "competition from foreign large-scale producers" and to increase the overall resilience of the agricultural sector, the Government of St Vincent and the Grenadines launched the Farmers Support Programme in February 2014.

The Farmers Support Programme makes loans available to farmers at an interest rate of 2 per cent, which is highly advantageous when compared with other agricultural loan financing institutions such as the St Vincent and the Grenadines Small Business and Micro-finance Co-operative Limited which lends at interest rates of 10 to 18 per cent on a reducing balance and the National Development Foundation which lends at a 9 per cent add-on interest rate. The programme also provides fertilizer and tools on credit to farmers.

The threat of an "ageing farming population and seeming lack of interest in farm labour" is being tackled by both the Government of St Vincent and the Grenadines and the Center for Enterprise Development, through their respective programmes, the Ministry of Agriculture Youth Summer Programme and the Agri-Business Summer Programme, which serve the threefold purpose of

1. increasing the interest of youth or younger persons in agriculture;
2. showing how new technology can be incorporated into farming; and
3. showing how to turn farming into a profitable venture.

The youth who participate in the programmes are taught in areas such as record-keeping, costing and pricing agricultural produce, marketing of agricultural produce, packaging and labelling, and good agricultural practices.

4.5 Factors Affecting St Vincent and the Grenadines' Competitiveness in the Food-Processing Sector

There are at least five factors affecting St Vincent and the Grenadines' competitiveness in the fruit and vegetable processing GVC. Each is outlined below along with a discussion of how these factors relate to VincyFresh. The section concludes with policy recommendations to address some of these shortcomings.

4.5.1 High Labour Cost

St Vincent and the Grenadines' labour force of fifty thousand persons represents 48 per cent of the population (103,220). The services, agriculture and industry sectors employ 57 per cent, 26 per cent and 16 per cent of the workforce, respectively (CIA 2013; CAIPA 2012). The minimum wage for unskilled industrial workers in St Vincent and the Grenadines is currently US$14.81 per day – for comparison, Jamaica has a minimum wage of US$11.21 per day, while the Dominican Republic has a minimum wage of US$4.60 per day.

VincyFresh currently exports its products to the Caribbean and Europe. However, judging by the significant difference in the minimum wage rate between the Dominican Republic and other Caribbean countries such as Jamaica and St Vincent and the Grenadines, should VincyFresh face direct competition from its neighbour, the Dominican Republic, it would have to compete on quality and not on price.

4.5.2 Infrastructure and Services

Since St Vincent and the Grenadines is an island, sea transportation is an important component of the country's infrastructure. However, sea transportation to neighbouring islands other than Trinidad and Tobago or Barbados is unreliable, and this increases the challenge of exporting to regional markets. St Vincent and the Grenadines had hoped to increase sea transportation to other neighbouring islands with the introduction of the fast ferry, but this service has proved to be insufficient.

VincyFresh sources its water from the Central Water and Sewerage Authority. However, the service is prone to interruption during the dry season, as well as during the "wet" or hurricane season when resulting landslides, and other disasters can burst water lines. It is therefore important for VincyFresh to have its own water treatment programme in the factory and invest in an alternative water source for processing.

Since St Vincent and the Grenadines is not an oil exporting country, the fuel charge associated with electricity is always an additional expense factor when oil prices rise on the global market.

4.5.3 Business Environment

St Vincent and the Grenadines is part of the eight-member Eastern Caribbean Currency Union. The union has a common currency, the Eastern Caribbean dollar that has been pegged to the US dollar at a fixed rate of EC$2.70 to

US$1.00 for the past thirty-seven years. The World Bank ranks St Vincent and the Grenadines 129 out of 185 global economies for the ease of getting credit (World Bank and IFCC 2013), which speaks to the fact that the country's banking system and bankruptcy laws do not provide strong support for small and medium businesses. Table 4.6 outlines the first three factors affecting the country's competitiveness.

4.5.4 Trade and Investment Policy

St Vincent and the Grenadines participates in several trade agreements that help to enhance the country's competitiveness (see table 4.7). It can benefit economically by leveraging the current trade agreements to achieve higher export earnings, increase employment, and improve its balance of trade through increased access to markets and the exemption from paying certain import duties.

For example, firms in CARICOM are afforded a protected market under the Revised Treaty of Chaguaramas, which addresses the deepening of the economic integration process through the establishment of the CARICOM Single Market and Economy.[5] St Vincent and the Grenadines is also a beneficiary of non-reciprocal preferential agreements with many industrialized countries under the generalized system of preferences. Under this arrangement, St Vincent and the Grenadines can export goods duty and quota free under unilaterally prescribed conditions (Bah 2009).[6]

The environment for investors in agro-processing is fairly attractive but needs to be further strengthened. Under the Fiscal Incentive Act, companies are granted concessions on goods and equipment for the manufacturing industry and can claim exemption on the importation of capital equipment and other components for production. In this regard, the Ministry of Agriculture is currently working with the customs department to provide equipment and input concessions for agro-processors.

As part of the modernization of the customs department, the introduction of the new customs software, Asycuda World, is expected to simplify procedures for clearance of goods and reduce processing times, helping to decrease inefficiencies.[7] The government has also established a trade facilitation committee charged with identifying and removing the barriers that inhibit the smooth flow of trade and business transactions.

The government's overall policies are geared towards enhancing the competitiveness of firms within the agro-processing industry through capacity-building

Table 4.6. Factors Affecting St Vincent and the Grenadines' Competitiveness (Part 1)

Factor		Description
Productive capacity and labour cost	Human capital	• Minimum wage for unskilled industrial workers – US$14.81 per day.
	Standards and certification	• The Ministry of Health and the St Vincent and the Grenadines Bureau of Standards are the regulators of mass producing food and beverages in St Vincent and the Grenadines. • Standards are not enforced by the regulators on the local supermarkets. • Labelling requirements are the standard which most local producers place emphasis on, since the Bureau of Standards' minimum requirement is that the date of manufacturing, best by date and the ingredients, along with nutritional value, be placed on every label in order for it to be sold on the local market. • Local producers do not place much emphasis on applying the local good manufacturing practice standards due to lack of information, lack of enforcement by the local authorities and lack of finances to implement the standards.
	National system of innovation	• The flow of technology and information among people is almost non-existent.
Infrastructure and services	Transportation, information communication technologies, energy and water	• Local ground transportation is readily available but expensive – due mainly to the high cost of fuel, the increase in import duties on vehicles and the high cost of capital. • Export by sea transportation to Trinidad and Barbados is readily available, due to active trade between these islands. • Export by sea transportation to other neighbouring islands is non-existent or irregular. • St Vincent and the Grenadines is currently serviced by one airline – LIAT. • Air transportation limitations are: high costs, limited direct flights to some destinations and limited capacity to carry a large volume of produce.

		- A large percentage of the population is computer literate.
- Internet access is available throughout the island, through a special project developed and maintained through the National Telecommunication Regulatory Commission.
- There are two Internet service providers – LIME and Karib Cable.
- Energy is purchased from the local electricity company, which depends on oil (80 per cent) as well as hydro sources to drive the production of electricity on the island.
- Water, which is supplied by the Central Water and Sewerage Authority, is generally reliable, usually well treated and good for human consumption.
Business environment	Macroeconomic stability and public governance	- GDP (PPP) of US$1.312 million (2012 est.)
- Unemployment rate: 18.8 per cent (2008)
- Inflation rate: 3.1 per cent (2012 est.)
- Stable exchange rate: US$1 = EC$2.70 since 1976
- Parliamentary democracy and constitutional monarchy
	Ease of opening a business and permitting/licensing	- Ease of Doing Business index rank: 75th among 185 countries globally.
- Ease of Starting a Business indicator rank: 64th among 185 countries globally.
- Starting a business: requires seven procedures, takes ten days, costs 17.9 per cent of income per capita and requires paid-in minimum capital of 0.0 per cent of income per capita.
	Access to finance	- Ease of Getting Credit indicator rank: 129 among 185 countries globally.
- Weak credit information system, collateral and bankruptcy laws.

Table 4.7. Current Trade Agreements

Caribbean Single Market and Economy	Economic Partnership Agreement*	Caribbean Basin Initiative	CARICOM Canada	Bilateral
CARICOM countries	European Community	United States	Canada	Costa Rica, Dominican Republic, Venezuela, Cuba, Colombia

* The Economic Partnership Agreement, which replaced the Contonou Agreement, was signed in 2008 between the European Union and twenty-seven African, Caribbean and Pacific countries. The Caribbean Single Market and Economy and the Economic Partnership Agreement provide firms within the agricultural sector with preferential access and a waiver of import duties on goods that are manufactured within CARICOM and are exported into other CARICOM countries and the European market.

Source: Bah 2009.

initiatives and by specific intervention for product development, marketing and export promotion. It has also signed an agreement with the Food and Agriculture Organization that is designed to improve the agricultural sector. This is supported by the Banana Adjustments Measures programme, which will enhance the value chain in the sector by improving the inbound and outbound logistics and the distribution and marketing of the products within the industry. The government also provides inputs for the agricultural industry at subsidized rates to farmers.

Table 4.8 outlines the final two factors affecting the country's competitiveness.

4.5.5 Institutionalization

VincyKlus Incorporated is the industry group and association that promotes the interests of agro-processors. The cluster group was established by the Center for Enterprise Development on 11 November 2010 with a view "to facilitate the growth and development of new and existing micro, small and medium enterprises in the agro-processing and service industries" (*VincyView* 2012). There are thirty-five members: twenty agro-processors and other professionals, including hoteliers and business support organizations.

According to Neisha Glasgow (interview, 10 June 2013),[8] the cluster has affected the production of fruits and vegetables in St Vincent and the Grenadines in a significant way. It has improved production of agro-processors by creating an awareness of branding, standards, promotion and access to markets.

Table 4.8. Factors Affecting St Vincent and the Grenadines' Competitiveness (Part 2)

Factor		Description
Trade and investment policy	Market access	• Bilateral trade agreements that offer zero tariffs on goods exported to the countries in CARICOM, the European market and other countries. • Import restrictions are imposed by several countries that demand adherence to international standards. • Bureau of Standards provides the technical support for the achievement of standards.
	Import tariffs	• Under the Fiscal Incentive Act, companies are granted concessions on goods and equipment for the manufacturing industry and can claim exemption on the importation of capital equipment and other components for production.
	Export-import procedures	• Reduced time for clearance of goods due to introduction of Asycuda World software. • Trade Facilitation Committee established by the government that is responsible for identifying and removing the barriers that inhibit the smooth flow of trade and business transactions.
	Industry-specific policies	• The Investment Promotion Agency has been given the mandate to promote export development. • The policies are geared towards enhancing the competitiveness of firms within the agro-processing industry through capacity building initiatives and by specific intervention for product development, marketing, and export promotion. • Government signed an agreement with the FAO designed to improve the agriculture sector from 2012 to 2015. • Banana Adjustments Measures programme will enhance the value chain in the sector by improving the inbound/outbound logistics and the distribution and marketing of the products within the industry. • Government provides the inputs into the agricultural industry at subsidized rates to the farmers.
Institutionalization	Industry maturity and coordination	• Key regulatory institutions: Ministry of Agriculture and the Bureau of Standards. • Main industry association: VincyKlus, registered and officially launched as a non-governmental organization in 2010. • Key chain actors present: agro-processors, hoteliers and business support organizations, such as the Centre for Enterprise Development.
	Public-private coordination	• Linkages and cooperation among private sector, government, educational institutions and other industry stakeholders is essential to rapidly identify and overcome challenges to chain participation.

Glasgow also stated that through VincyKlus, cluster members have had access to more information through workshops, participation in trade shows, exhibitions and consultations. The cluster has also facilitated the training of professionals in strategy and development. Additionally, the organization has advocated for technical assistance on behalf of its membership.

Interviews with other prominent stakeholders in the agriculture and agro-processing industry revealed that while several public and private institutions provide support to the sector, deeper linkages and collaborations need to take place among actors in order to identify and overcome St Vincent and the Grenadines' challenges to sustainable participation in the fruit and vegetable processing GVC. The institutions that are considered critical to the development and expansion of the fruit and vegetable sector in the country are the Ministry of Trade, Ministry of Agriculture, Bureau of Standards, Invest St Vincent and the Grenadines, Center for Enterprise Development Incorporated, Chamber of Industry and Commerce and the Windward Islands Farmers Association (Glasgow interview, 2013).

4.6 Lessons Learned

Lesson 1: Exporting companies need to ensure that they have a consistent and adequate supply of quality fruits and vegetables in order to remain competitive.

In 2011, VincyFresh asked small producers in St Vincent and the Grenadines to supply peppers for the manufacture of its pepper-based products. Many small farmers responded, and pepper production exceeded VincyFresh's processing needs. Since VincyFresh did not enter into formal contracts to buy the peppers from the small farmers, many of them suffered losses because the company did not purchase all of the peppers produced; in turn, the farmers could not find markets to sell their excess peppers (interview with Kemston Cato, 1 June 2013). Since then, VincyFresh has faced challenges in sourcing consistent and sufficiently large quantities of fruits and vegetables due to fears of overproduction by farmers. The company has now realized that it must enter into contractual arrangements with small producers if it is to ensure a consistent supply of quantity and quality.

Lesson 2: A more efficient and robust business model is needed if VincyFresh is to achieve sustained export competitiveness.

The current model is not competitive since it is plagued with management problems, financial challenges, capacity and production difficulties, and state control. The company needs to take a look at its facilities to ascertain how well they would function with the current Hazard Analysis and Critical Control Points plan that is to be implemented.

Lesson 3: Clustering produces synchronous benefits for small producers, which helps the country and the region.

The cluster framework can be a valuable tool for effective economic change because it is market driven, inclusive, collaborative, strategic and value creating (World Bank 2011). The VincyKlus industry association, of which VincyFresh is a member, has already helped deliver some of these benefits by providing support for members. More support for members is needed, however, and this can be obtained, as will be outlined in recommendation six below.

Through its various initiatives, VincyKlus has also become more market driven – improving the production of agro-processors by creating an awareness of branding, standards, promotion and access to markets.

4.7 Upgrading Recommendations for VincyFresh

VincyFresh can improve its position in fruit and vegetable processing GVCs by making enhancements that follow the concept of upgrading outlined in the GVC literature. Upgrading has been defined as the activities or strategies that are used by a firm, country, region, or economic stakeholder to improve its position or competitiveness in the global economy (Gereffi and Fernandez-Stark 2011).

Upgrading, "which is innovation to increase value added", is a necessary condition for a "high road" path to competitiveness in the context of globalization – increase and improve participation in the international economy, and ensure a sustainable growth of per capita incomes (Pietrobelli and Rabellotti 2004).

Humphrey and Schmitz (2002, quoted in Gereffi and Fernandez-Stark 2011) define the following four types of upgrading strategies and tactics in GVCs:

1. Process upgrading: Transforming inputs into outputs more efficiently by reorganizing the production system or introducing superior technology.
2. Product upgrading: Moving into more sophisticated product lines (which can be defined in terms of increased unit values).
3. Functional upgrading: Acquiring new functions (or abandoning existing functions) to increase the overall skill content of activities.
4. Inter-sectoral upgrading: Firms of clusters move into new productive activities.

4.7.1 Process Upgrade: Invest in Capital Improvements

Washing and peeling of fruits and vegetables for processing at VincyFresh is currently done manually and takes a longer time than if it were automated. Additionally, the machinery used in the processing segment for drying, freezing, preserving and making juices and pulps is usually left idle for longer than necessary. VincyFresh should introduce mechanized washing and peeling into its operations in order to transform its inputs (fruits and vegetables) into outputs (dried, frozen and preserved products, juices and pulps) more efficiently. This will allow the company to process more fruits and vegetables in any given period, increase productivity and reduce the handling and possible sanitary violations in its operations.

4.7.2 Product Upgrade: Move Into "Ready-to-Eat" Product Lines

Busier lifestyles have created an increasing class of customers who are looking for "ready-to-eat" solutions. Therefore, VincyFresh could explore moving into this "more sophisticated" product line of "ready-to-eat" fruits and vegetables, particularly for the international market. VincyFresh also has a great opportunity to create convenience with its vacuum-packed foods by not only improving their labelling but also by including recipes on their labels. This can be explored with their pre-packed vegetables.

4.7.3 Inter-sectoral Upgrade: Deepen Collaboration and Linkages among Key Investors in Capital Improvements

As was mentioned earlier, interviews with prominent stakeholders in the agriculture and agro-processing industry revealed the need for deeper linkages and collaborations among key actors in the fruit and vegetable sector in St Vincent and the Grenadines.

Seven specific organizations were identified by those stakeholders as being critical to the development and expansion of the fruit and vegetable sector in St Vincent and the Grenadines. It is important to note that five of the seven identified organizations were government-related entities – the Ministry of Trade, Ministry of Agriculture, Bureau of Standards, Invest St Vincent and the Grenadines and the Center for Enterprise Development Incorporated.

Since there is advantage to be gained in numbers, VincyFresh should proactively approach those identified key government actors through its umbrella association VincyKlus, in order to deal with challenges that are common to the cluster members. The resolution of those challenges would then benefit VincyFresh.

In order to achieve these upgrades and determine other upgrading opportunities not identified in this report, VincyFresh should employ the following short, medium and long-term strategies.

4.7.4 Recommendation 1 (Short-term): Lead the Collaborative Strategy at VincyKlus

"Empirical data that has become available in recent years has confirmed the strong link between clusters and economic performance" (Ketels 2008). In order to achieve cluster-based economic development, however, a summary of two studies reveals that a four-stage process is required:

- Stage 1: Mobilization – building interest and participation among the different constituencies needed to carry out the initiative.
- Stage 2: Diagnosis – assessing the industry clusters that comprise the economy and the economic infrastructure that supports cluster performance.
- Stage 3: Collaborative Strategy – convening demand-side stakeholders (companies in each cluster) and supply-side stakeholders (public and private supporting economic institutions) in working groups to identify priority challenges and action initiatives to address shared problems.
- Stage 4: Implementation – building the commitment of cluster working group participants and regional stakeholders to actions and identifying or creating an organization to sustain implementation (World Bank 2011).

Additionally, according to Ketels (2008), although many benefits of clusters can occur purely because of co-location, "purposive collaboration can enhance the ability of clusters to drive higher economic performance and innovation". Consequently, "companies in cluster with strong cooperation can better exploit the complementary skills and capabilities of local suppliers and service providers" and are "often better placed to turn business environment advantages into competitive advantages" (ibid.).

VincyKlus has, to a large extent, already worked its way through stages 1 and 2 but needs to make significant strides in reaching stage 3 – collaborative strategy.

As an exporter, VincyFresh is a crucial link between producers and suppliers in the local market and the buyers of fresh and processed fruits and vegetables, both regionally and internationally. VincyFresh should, therefore, take up a strategic lead position to actively assist producers within the VincyKlus cluster, with meeting international quality standards, keeping up-to-date on quality standards, adapting to new changing standards, identifying priority challenges for demand-side and supply-side stakeholders and implementing best-practice action initiatives that will address and solve their shared challenges.

Through this sustained support to and collaboration with producers and farmers, VincyFresh can actively monitor and build commitment to quality, which will have positive implications for consistency in the quality and quantity of fruits and vegetables supplied to the company. By extension, this will result in the sustained strengthening of the agro-processing cluster.

4.7.5 Recommendation 2 (Short-, Medium- and Long-Term): Intensify Continuous Workforce Training

This case study reveals that thus far VincyFresh has engaged in some on-the-job and external training initiatives for its workforce in food handling, hygiene and fire drills. Since "standards training today is a basic requirement to compete in high-value markets" (Fernandez-Stark, Bamber and Gereffi 2011), the company needs to engage in ongoing training of its workforce in food handling and safety, as well as other relevant fruit and vegetable standards in order to meet ever-changing global standards requirements and remain competitive.

4.7.6 Recommendation 3 (Short-Term): Undertake a Comprehensive Market Analysis

VincyFresh needs to conduct market analysis in order to determine the specific market strategies for each of its targeted segments, including product definition and destination. For example, even on the local market there are approximately fifteen different brands of the green seasonings. Does it make sense to add another brand or should local producers pursue contract packaging? Market intelligence can dictate to the company how it should streamline its products and what its marketing strategy should be for each one.

4.7.7 Recommendation 4 (Medium- to Long-Term): Build a Collaborative Relationship with Key Government Actors through VincyKlus

Since many of the challenges experienced by VincyFresh are systemic and not limited to VincyFresh, it might be useful to actively work towards establishing a collaborative relationship with the Government of St Vincent and the Grenadines' through VincyKlus, since the government is the entity best positioned to effect change.

Lobbying for the following policies and policy changes may help to support the competitiveness of VincyFresh and other firms in the fruit and vegetable processing GVCs:

- Providing access to export finance through the establishment of financing services that will enable small and medium-sized enterprises to compete by reducing credit risks and by providing working capital.
- Strengthening the marketing and research capabilities of the state agency that has been designated to provide export development services. This would allow it to provide information on trade policy, trade facilitation, market information and intelligence, and export promotion activities.
- Accelerating the implementation of the Small Business Development Bill that will provide institutional support for the agribusiness industry by providing incentives and tax deductions.
- Changing the import licence requirement policies for a number of agricultural products to ensure consistent supply of raw materials for processing plants.
- Facilitating the establishment of a cooperative within the agribusiness industry with the goal of providing access to financing for small farmers.
- Establishing a modern processing facility that is designed to provide value-added products.

4.7.8 Recommendation 5 (Medium- to Long-Term): Expand Exports and Export Quantities

VincyFresh's continuous operating losses and underutilized plant operating capacity (30 to 40 per cent utilization) (Cato interview, 2013) support the idea that the company needs to expand its exports, as well as its export quantities.

In terms of exporters, there are opportunities that VincyFresh should explore in order to

- increase its exports in all five product categories to the United States and the United Kingdom where it already exports, especially since there is no current quota for the export of fresh produce to the European market and both the United States and the United Kingdom are English-speaking countries;
- explore new export opportunities with Canada, which is a lead importer of sauces and seasonings and frozen fruits, and also an English-speaking country;
- explore untapped export opportunities with France and Germany, which are lead importers of sauces and seasonings, jams and jellies, fruit juices and frozen fruits; and
- explore untapped export opportunities with China and Japan, which are lead importers of roots and tubers.

Additionally, it should also be noted that in the case of sauces and seasonings and jams and jellies, some of the lead importers, such as the United Kindom, the United States, Germany and France, are also lead exporters in similar or greater quantity. Specific export opportunities also exist for VincyFresh in the following areas, where the import share of each country is significantly higher than its export share:

- Fruit juices: United States (exports 8 per cent; imports 13 per cent)
- Fruit juices: Germany (exports 7 per cent; imports 11 per cent)
- Fruit juices: Netherlands (exports 8 per cent; imports 12 per cent)
- Roots and tubers: China (exports 12 per cent; imports 44 per cent)

Additionally, once VincyFresh has made significant headway in the implementation of recommendations 1 through 4, in order to increase its profitability, it should also increase its overall export quantities of the company's current product lines through a three-pronged approach/strategy:

1. Market and expand in its current export markets (Antigua, Tortola, Barbados, Grenada, Trinidad, Dominica, the United Kingdom and the United States) with its current product lines.
2. Enter into target markets (British Virgin Islands) with its current product lines.

3. Market and enter unconventional markets (the Netherlands, France, Germany, China and Japan) that are lead importers of products that VincyFresh currently manufactures. These target countries have traditionally been ignored, primarily due to difference in language.

This language barrier can be surmounted through a combination of the following strategies:

1. Recruit persons with both agricultural qualifications and experience as well as language competence in French, Dutch, German, Chinese and Japanese.
2. Incentivize the existing staff to extend their language skills to include those languages.
3. Encourage the government to pursue more agricultural scholarships to those countries. Between 2002 and 2013, sixty-three students benefited from Republic of China (Taiwan) scholarships in diverse areas, including agriculture, which makes this option very feasible (Embassy of the Republic of China [Taiwan] in St Vincent and the Grenadines 2013).

Particular attention should be given to using the Netherlands as another entry point into Europe, since "the Netherlands is the biggest importer from outside the EU with almost 2.6 million tons of fruit and 367 thousand tons of vegetables. [Additionally], ports in the Netherlands and Belgium share many years of experience with fresh produce, holding a strong position as entry points into mainland Europe", mainly due to their logistical positioning (CBI 2015).

4.7.9 Recommendation 6 (Medium- to Long-Term): Build Collaborative Relationships with Large Global Supermarkets

Although a decline in global market prices for agro-products threatens to negatively impact the sustainability of the industry (see table 4.5), there has been a growing niche demand for fresh fruits and vegetables.

According to the Centre for the Promotion of Imports from Developing Countries (CBI 2015), "Fresh fruit and vegetables are one of the most important categories in European supermarkets with total import volume of fresh fruit and fresh vegetables from outside the European Union at 11 million tons (almost

€10 billion) and 2.1 million tons (€2.2 billion), respectively". The Centre for the Promotion of Imports also noted that "Import growth is most clearly seen in the increasing popularity of tropical products (e.g., avocados and mangos), as well as for niche products (e.g., berries and exotic fruit and vegetables)."

Caribbean exporters such as VincyFresh need to continuously observe what is happening in the fruit and vegetable GVC in order to understand where power resides in the chain and make swift and strategic moves. One key observation that Fernandez-Stark, Bamber and Gereffi made in their 2011 study is that large supermarket chains such as Sainsbury's, Marks and Spencer, and Walmart, have become the leading actors in key export markets with controlling market shares in the European Union, the United States and emerging markets. These supermarket buyers seek product differentiation and are often interested in unique offerings such as "ready-to-eat" meals.

Consequently, VincyFresh should expand its product offerings to include "ready-to-eat" or "ready-to-cook" alternatives for large global supermarkets, once it has made significant headway in the implementation of recommendations one through five.

Notes

1. "Black sigatoka is a leaf-spot disease affecting banana plants caused by the ascomycete fungus" (Wikipedia http://en.wikipedia.org/wiki/Black_sigatoka).
2. The fruit and vegetable processing industry involves food products that are packaged in jars and cans, bottled, preserved, quick-frozen or dried.
3. Dasheen is an edible root vegetable or tuber (also known as taro) that is grown and used in many Caribbean, African, Oceanic and South Indian countries as part of the common diet.
4. "[t]he CARICOM Single Market and Economy is intended to benefit the people of the Region by providing more and better opportunities to produce and sell our goods and services and to attract investment" (CARICOM 2011).
5. The Caribbean Single Market and Economy, which was signed into law by St Vincent and the Grenadines in 2005, forms part of the Revised Treaty of Chaguaramas that established the Caribbean Community and Common Market (CARICOM) in 1973.
6. These countries include Australia, Bulgaria, Canada, the Czech Republic, the European Union, Hungary, Japan, New Zealand, Norway, Poland, Russia, the Slovak Republic, Switzerland and the United States.
7. Asycuda World is web-based software that automates web transactions for customs officials and traders. It is provided by the United Nations Conference on Trade and Development to countries around the world at no cost.

8. Business development officer at the Centre for Enterprise Development Inc. and secretary to VincyKlus Inc.

References

Bah, G. 2009. *St Vincent and the Grenadines Trade Policy Framework: The Fostering of a Modern Competitive Postcolonial Economy in SVG*. St Vincent and the Grenadines: Ministry of Foreign Affairs and Trade.

BBC. 2013. "St Vincent and the Grenadines: Banana Farmers 'Abandoning Fields'". News from Elsewhere, 6 August. http://www.bbc.com/news/blogs-news-from-elsewhere-23590747.

CAIPA (Caribbean Association of Investment Promotion Agencies). 2012. "SVG Invest Country Profile: St Vincent and the Grenadines". Accessed 24 October 2014. http://caipainvest.org/members-ipas/st-vincent-and-the-grenadines.html.

CARICOM. 2011. "The CARICOM Single Market and Economy (CSME)". Accessed 24 October 2014. http://caricom.org/jsp/single_market/single_market_index.jsp?menu=csme.

CBI (Centre for the Promotion of Imports from Developing Countries). 2015. "CBI Trade Statistics: Fresh Fruit and Vegetables in Europe". *Market Intelligence*. https://www.cbi.eu/sites/default/files/trade-statistics-europe-fresh-fruit-vegetables-2015.pdf.

CIA (Central Intelligence Agency). 2013. *World Fact Book*. https://www.cia.gov/library/publications/the-world-factbook/geos/vc.html.

Embassy of the Republic of China (Taiwan) in St Vincent and the Grenadines. 2013. Taiwanese Scholarships Available to Vincentian Youths Now. Accessed 24 October 2014. http://www.taiwanembassy.org/content.asp?mp=727&CuItem=353051.

Fernandez-Stark, K., P. Bamber and G. Gereffi. 2011. *The Fruit and Vegetables Global Value Chain: Economic Upgrading and Workforce Development*. Durham, NC: Duke University Center on Globalization, Governance and Competitiveness. http://www.cggc.duke.edu/pdfs/2011-11-10_CGGC_Fruit-and-Vegetables-Global-Value-Chain.pdf.

First Research. 2013. "Fruit and Vegetable Processing Industry Profile". Accessed 24 October 2014. http://www.firstresearch.com/industry-research/Fruit-and-Vegetable-Processing.html.

Gereffi, G., and K. Fernandez-Stark. 2011. *Global Value Chain Analysis: A Primer*. Durham, NC: Duke University Center on Globalization, Governance and Competitiveness. http://www.cggc.duke.edu/pdfs/2011-05-31_GVC_analysis_a_primer.pdf.

ICDF (International Cooperation and Development Fund). 2013. "St Vincent and the Grenadines". Accessed 11 September 2014.

IMF (International Monetary Fund). 2011. "St Vincent and the Grenadines: 2011 Article IV Consultation". Accessed 24 October 2014. http://www.imf.org/external/pubs/ft/scr/2011/cr11343.pdf.

Ketels, C.H.M. 2008. "From Clusters to Cluster-Based Economic Development". Accessed 17 February 2015. http://ibr.hi.is/sites/ibr.hi.is/files/From_clusters_to_cluster_based_economic_development.pdf.

Pietrobelli, C., and R. Rabellotti. 2004. "Competitiveness and Upgrading in Clusters and Value Chains: The Case of Latin America". Accessed 24 October 2014. http://www.slideshare.net/Annie05/competitiveness-and-upgrading-in-clusters-and-value-chains-presentation.

Report Linker. 2013. "Fruit and Vegetable Trends: Top Changes Impacting the Market". Accessed 24 October 2014. http://www.reportlinker.com/ci02029/Fruit-and-Vegetable.html.

SVG–EU (St Vincent and the Grenadines–European Commission). 2002. St Vincent and the Grenadines–European Community Country Strategy Paper and National Indicative Programme for the period 2002–2007. http://www.unicef.org/lac/spbarbados/Planning/national/St.Vincent%20and%20the%20Grenadines/EU_vc_csp_en.pdf.

———. 2008. St Vincent and the Grenadines–European Community: Country Strategy Paper and National Indicative Programme for the Period 2008–2013 (10th EDF). https://ec.europa.eu/europeaid/sites/devco/files/csp-nip-st-vincent-grenadines-2008-2013_en.pdf.

Vincy View. 2012. "This Country's Lone Agro-processing Cluster Group, VincyKlus Is Now Equipped to Start the Basic Functions of Its Secretariat". Accessed 24 October 2014. http://vincyview.com/2012/05/16/this-country%E2%80%99s-lone-agro-processing-cluster-group-vincyklus-is-now-equipped-to-start-the-basic-functions-of-its-secretariat/.

World Bank. 2011. "Doing Cluster Analysis". Accessed 24 October 2014. http://web.worldbank.org/WBSITE/EXTERNAL/TOPICS/EXTURBANDEVELOPMENT/EXTLED/0,,contentMDK:20274518~menuPK:341145~pagePK:148956~piPK:216618~theSitePK:341139,00.html.

World Bank and IFCC (International Finance Corporation). 2013. Doing Business 2013: Smarter Regulations for Small and Medium-Size Enterprises. Accessed 23 October 2014. http://doingbusiness.org/reports/global-reports/doing-business-2013.

Appendix 4.1. VincyFresh Organizational Chart

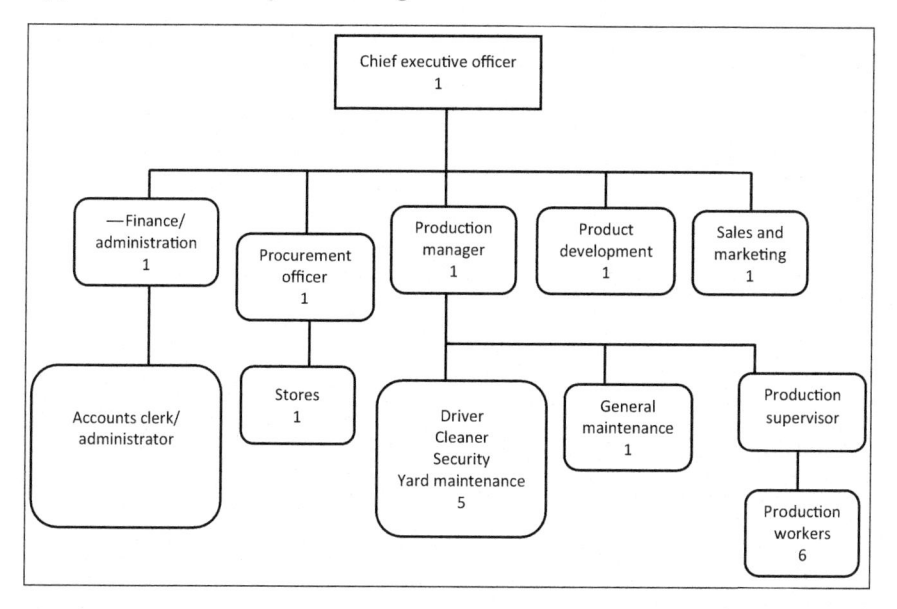

- Chief executive officer (1)
  - Finance/administration (1)
    - Accounts clerk/administrator
  - Procurement officer (1)
    - Stores (1)
  - Production manager (1)
    - Driver, Cleaner, Security, Yard maintenance (5)
  - Product development (1)
    - General maintenance (1)
  - Sales and marketing (1)
    - Production supervisor
      - Production workers (6)

Source: VincyFresh Limited.

Section 2
Services Industry Case Studies

CASE STUDY 5

The Chaguaramas Ship Repair Cluster
Sustaining Competitiveness and Lessons for Upgrading Along the Maritime Value Chain

DON CHARLES
PhD Student
Department of Economics
University of the West Indies, St Augustine

DEBBIE A. MOHAMMED
Senior Lecturer
Institute of International Relations and Arthur Lok Graduate School of Business
University of the West Indies, St Augustine

PREEYA MOHAN
Postdoctoral Research Fellow
Sir Arthur Lewis Institute of Social and Economic Studies
University of the West Indies, St Augustine

Abstract

The Government of the Republic of Trinidad and Tobago has identified ship repair as one of seven sectors for diversification of the economy. While ship repair is a relatively new area of focus for the government, the country has long been engaged in the commercial repair of vessels particularly in Chaguaramas, located in the north-western peninsula of Trinidad. The Chaguaramas ship repair cluster is primarily driven by the private sector, highly profitable and attracts local, regional and international clients. The country's ideal location between key trade routes, favourable climate and exchange rate, political stability and years of experience in this industry, make ship repair an excellent candidate for economic diversification. The success of the Chaguaramas cluster to date provides an opportunity for its further expansion and development, as well as to serve as a model for replicating these successes at other ports in the country in line with the government's development plans, possibly using the public-private partnership model.

5.1 Introduction

The economy of Trinidad and Tobago is driven primarily by the oil and gas industry and its related downstream activities. In 2013, the energy sector, which is made up of oil, natural gas, refining and downstream petrochemicals, accounted for 42.9 per cent of the Trinidad and Tobago's gross domestic product and 81 per cent of merchandise exports (Central Bank of Trinidad and Tobago 2013). In an effort to diversify the economy and ensure a more competitive and sustainable growth path, the government has identified the maritime industry and specifically ship repair as a strategic cluster, believing it has the potential to increase foreign direct investment. The ship repair sector complements Trinidad and Tobago's offshore hydrocarbon sector by providing maintenance support for activities upstream and midstream (for example, exploration and processing) and downstream (for example, transshipment). The Chaguaramas ship repair cluster could also provide other benefits, including presenting an opportunity to apply more fully the public-private partnership model that was identified by the government as a means of growing the industry. Finally, the cluster could serve as a best-practice model for the development of new clusters in other ports targeted by the government, such as Sea Lots, Point Lisas and La Brea.

5.2 Overview of the Chaguaramas Cluster

Trinidad and Tobago has two international standard container ports, one liquefied natural gas (LNG) terminal, one bauxite transshipment facility, one petrochemical port, and one port for an oil refinery (InvesTT 2012). The port in Port of Spain currently receives the majority of the country's bulk cargo vessels and marine vessels involved in transshipment. Since marine vessels periodically need repair and maintenance services, the presence of ports and their associated marine traffic encouraged the development of Trinidad and Tobago's ship repair cluster in the Chaguaramas peninsula.

The Chaguaramas ship repair cluster is located in the north-western peninsula of Trinidad, just west of the city's capital, Port of Spain. It is highly profitable and is populated mostly by private sector actors. The cluster is dominated by four major dry-docking facilities: Caribbean Dockyard and Engineering Services Limited, a subsidiary of CL Marine which has been taken over by the Government of the Republic of Trinidad and Tobago; Interisle Construction and Fabricating Company Limited; Crews In; and Peake Yacht Services. These facilities rely on a network of small firms to provide highly specialized related and supporting services which may not be readily available in-house, or may be unavailable in the quantities required for specific jobs. Some of these related and supporting service firms are located within the geographic cluster and others are dispersed across the island. Each of these four companies provides services for distinct segments of the marine market. CL Marine handles Panama-sized vessels (ocean liners, oil tankers), Interisle specializes in medium-sized vessels (supply vessels and launches), while Peake Yacht Services and Crews In focus on smaller ships, including fishing vessels, tugs and pleasure boats. These four companies compete among themselves and with regional providers for dry-docking services in the Atlantic region.

Given the sector's capital intensity and the specialized knowledge required, these four main companies exert the most power and influence in the ship repair industry. Figure 5.1 provides an overview of the major companies in the Chaguaramas ship repair cluster.

Supplier firms include the many small providers of specialized services to the four main players. The goods and services provided by these smaller businesses include welding and fabrication, painting and blasting, chandelling, brokerage, freight forwarding and marine insurance. Given that there are many small service suppliers, the four large dry-dock companies exert power over these suppliers in demanding competitive prices, high quality and timely service. On the demand side, customers consist of local, regional and international clients. These consumers demand high quality and competitive prices given the number of dry-docking companies available – only in the case of an emergency would customers be forced to go with a specific company and not pursue the lowest price.

The government is another important stakeholder in the maritime cluster. In addition to being responsible for policy and legislation, the government – specifically, the Ministry of Trade, Industry, Investment and Communications – has identified the maritime sector as a key sector for diversification of the economy. In addition, the government has partnered with the University of Trinidad and Tobago to establish specialized training programmes to increase the pool of skilled labour for the maritime sector.

Other stakeholders of the maritime cluster include the Environmental Management Authority, which enforces local environmental protections, the Maritime Services of Trinidad and Tobago, a division of the Ministry of Works and Transport, which regulates matters relating to the maritime industry, the

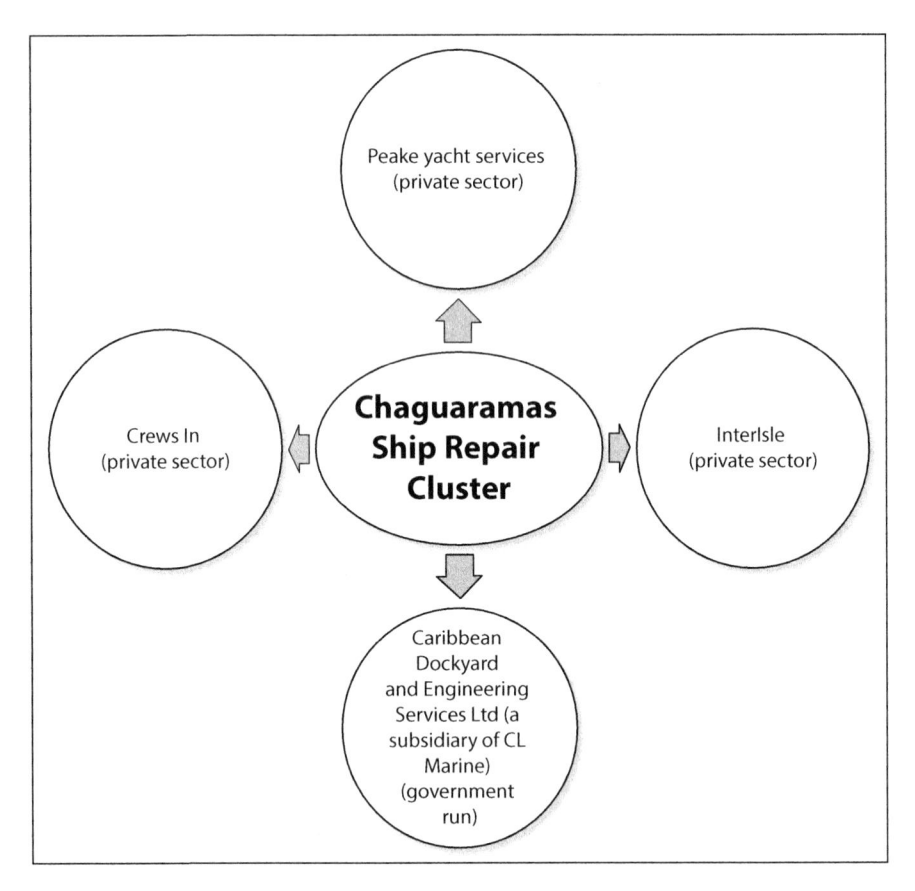

Figure 5.1. Key companies of the Chaguaramas ship repair cluster
Source: Authors' compilation.

agencies that enforce industry standards (local and foreign), and the owners of marine vessels that require repair services. Additionally, there are shipping agents, ship brokers and freight forwarders. Lastly, the Shipping Association of Trinidad and Tobago is an association that represents the interests of key industry stakeholders.

5.3 The Global Ship Repair Industry

Ship repair and shipbuilding have traditionally been performed in the same locations because of similarities in capital and labour requirements. As a result, some of the world leaders in shipbuilding are also the leaders in ship repair, although there are some yards that only focus on one activity. Whereas shipbuilding is the design and construction of new vessels and often takes more than a year to complete, ship repair occurs in a much shorter time frame (usually ten to twelve days) and involves activities such as general repair of parts, breakdowns, conversions and maintenance (OECD 2008). These activities must conform to strict international safety standards.

Countries in Europe have historically dominated the shipbuilding and repair industry. However, new competitors have emerged, including China, India, Japan, Dubai, Bahrain, Sri Lanka, Singapore, South Korea, the Philippines and Vietnam.[1] Singapore is the leading ship repair centre, controlling approximately 20 per cent of global market sales, followed by Dubai, Bahrain and Sri Lanka (CESA 2011). European countries still account for 35 per cent of the industry, although this figure is expected to fall in the future given the shift to lower-cost countries (ibid.). The emergence of these new centres can be attributed to their favourable location along trade routes and lower labour costs (Mickeviciene 2011).

The forecasted global growth of the ship repair industry between 2007 and 2015 was 110 per cent (OECD 2008). This can be attributed to an increase in the global fleet and the fact that the increased complexity of modern ships required more regular maintenance and inspections. This translated to annual sales of the ship repair industry of US$10–12 billion in 2007 (ibid.).

Dominant features of the global shipbuilding industry are the increase in demand for new ships and their shortage of supply, which has profound implications for the Trinidad and Tobago ship repair industry. Since global demand exceeds supply, older ships must stay in operation longer, thereby increasing the need for repair services. In response to this demand, many marine and dry-docking companies are seeking to increase their supply of services.

5.4 The Regional Ship Repair Industry

In the Atlantic region, there are several dry docks that can accommodate marine vessels larger than 300 metres (*Trinidad and Tobago Shipbuilder and Repair News*, no. 7, 2008). Curaçao currently has the largest dry-dock facility in the entire Caribbean region, and Curaçao Drydock Company, one of the largest companies in the region, can perform both ship repair and shipbuilding services (*Caribbean Maritime* 2012). Table 5.1 lists the dry docks in the region that serve as competition for Trinidad and Tobago. Although countries such as

Table 5.1. Number of Docks in the Caribbean That Can Accommodate Vessels Larger Than 300 Metres

Location	Number of Yards
Bayonne, NJ, United States	1
Boston, MA, United States	1
Brooklyn, NY, United States	2
Columbia	1
Curaçao	3
Freeport, Grand Bahama, Bahamas	1
Grenada	1
Newport News, VA, United States	2
Norfolk, VA, United States	1
Panama	1
Philadelphia, United States	2
Rio de Janeiro, Brazil	1
Roslindale, MA, United States	1
Trinidad and Tobago	1

Source: *Trinidad and Tobago Shipbuilder and Repair News*, no. 7 (2008), http://issuu.com/shipbuildingandrepair; Curaçao Drydock Company, http://www.ruta-curacao.com/index.php?page-id=5&show=news&news_id=13.

Panama, the Bahamas and Colombia possess only one shipyard, they pose competitive challenges for Trinidad and Tobago because of their modern facilities and their capacity to accommodate vessels larger than 300 metres.

Additionally, there are multiple smaller shipyards in Curaçao, Colombia and Grenada which can accommodate marine vessels smaller than 300 metres that also engage in both ship repair and shipbuilding.

5.5 The Ship Repair Global Value Chain

The global value chain (GVC) for the ship repair industry is made up of ship repair and ship conversion (figure 5.2). Ship repair refers to all the repair and maintenance activities for marine vessels. Ship conversion refers to the modification work necessary to change marine vehicles into another type of vessel.

Because ship repair is labour intensive, it is an attractive industry for developing countries looking to create jobs and strengthen economic growth.

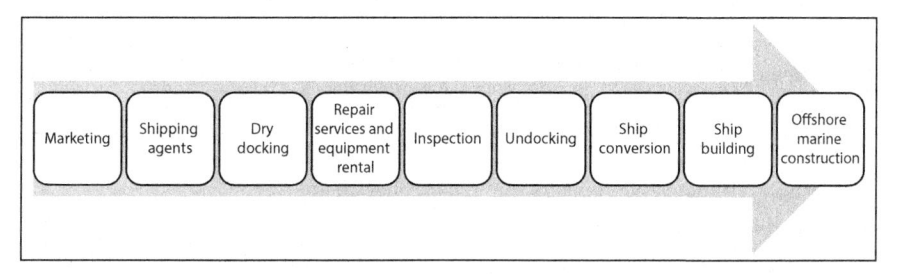

Figure 5.2. Ship repair global value chain
Source: Authors' compilation.

However, it should be noted that this segment requires specialized and highly skilled labour, which, regardless of location (developed or developing country), commands high wages. In terms of competitiveness, one of the main challenges for Trinidad and Tobago is competition based on cost. High labour costs are not necessarily accompanied by commensurate productivity, and high prices for repairs are sometimes the result of the inflated cost of the imported replacement parts. This is compounded by inefficiencies at major ports, which lead to delays and further cost increases since shipyards must pay clients for any delays.

Despite these challenges, the industry is poised for growth. Much of this can be attributed to the increase in the global fleet; from 1990 to 2011, dead weight tonnage increased from 660 million to 1.46 billion, a jump of 122 per cent (CESA 2011). This provides demand conditions that support the expansion of the global ship repair industry.

5.5.1 Trinidad and Tobago in the Ship Repair Global Value Chain

Trinidad and Tobago's ship repair cluster is relatively insignificant when compared to large players such as Singapore, South Korea, China, Japan and countries in Europe, particularly in segments such as ship conversion and shipbuilding (figure 5.3). Notwithstanding this, the sector has the potential to make a noteworthy contribution to the country's economy, both in terms of ship repair – which is the major focus of the industry's activities – and higher value-added activities such as shipbuilding.

According to de Gannes (2010), the ship repair industry contributes an estimated US$17 million annually to gross domestic product and creates more than

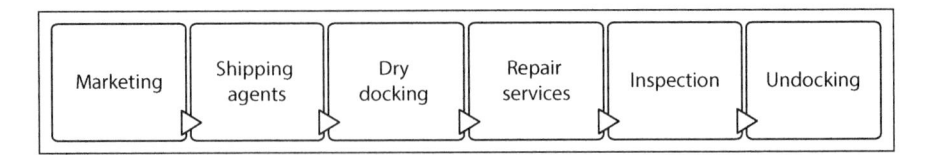

Marketing → Shipping agents → Dry docking → Repair services → Inspection → Undocking

Figure 5.3. Trinidad and Tobago's ship repair value chain
Source: Authors' compilation.

350 direct jobs. To put this industry's contribution in context, the gross domestic product of Trinidad and Tobago in 2013 was US$24,596.5 million (CSO 2013).[2] Therefore, the ship repair industry contributed less than 1 per cent to Trinidad and Tobago's gross domestic product. In terms of contribution to employment, the labour force in 2012 was 678,521 (World Bank 2014), with the ship repair industry employing 0.05 per cent of the labour force. While this might appear small, it is noteworthy that the marine industries in Trinidad and Tobago have a high multiplier effect – for every $1 spent in the industry, it generates $5 of economic benefit for the overall economy (de Gannes 2010).

While Trinidad and Tobago is not recognized globally as a ship repair hub, the industry benefits from its strategic location close to North America, Europe and the Panama Canal. Trinidad and Tobago's proximity to key trade routes provides a captive market for ship repair services. Quality of service at a competitive price has been identified as a significant factor in getting repeat and pre-planned routine maintenance (de Gannes and Persad 2010).

Since a significant amount of demand for ship repair services is unscheduled and depends on external factors, assessing the future demand for ship repair services is difficult. Trinidad and Tobago's government must be aware of this volatility as it attempts to boost the contribution of the Chaguaramas cluster to the national economy. Encouragingly, Trinidad and Tobago's ship repair sector has developed certain core competencies (figure 5.4), particularly in marine engineering and related skill sets that may provide the basis for building a more realistic value chain for the country's ship repair industry (interviews with staff of Interisle, 2013). While moving up the value chain can include expanding into shipbuilding, capacity constraints, both human and infrastructural, will make this difficult. Emphasis should therefore be placed on improving the activity that the cluster does best – ship repair – and it may be useful to focus on increasing the number and quality of skilled persons in higher value-added activities such as project management, job costing, and health and safety. Trinidad and Tobago

Activities

Fresh-water pressure washing Sandblasting Painting Grit blasting	Fabrication Welding Steel repairs Machinery repairs Gas-free certification Shipwright Glass repairs	Construction Waterfront structural Engineering Electrical and electronics

Marine equipment rentals Remote location repairs	Underwater services In-transit repairs	Wet dock repairs Waste management	Inspection Chandler

Actors

Small service providers Freight forwarders	Shipping agents Governmental agencies Educational institutions	Ship brokers SATT

Services

Dry docking and docking facilities	⇨ Construction and repair ⇨	Marine engineering

Increasing value ⇨

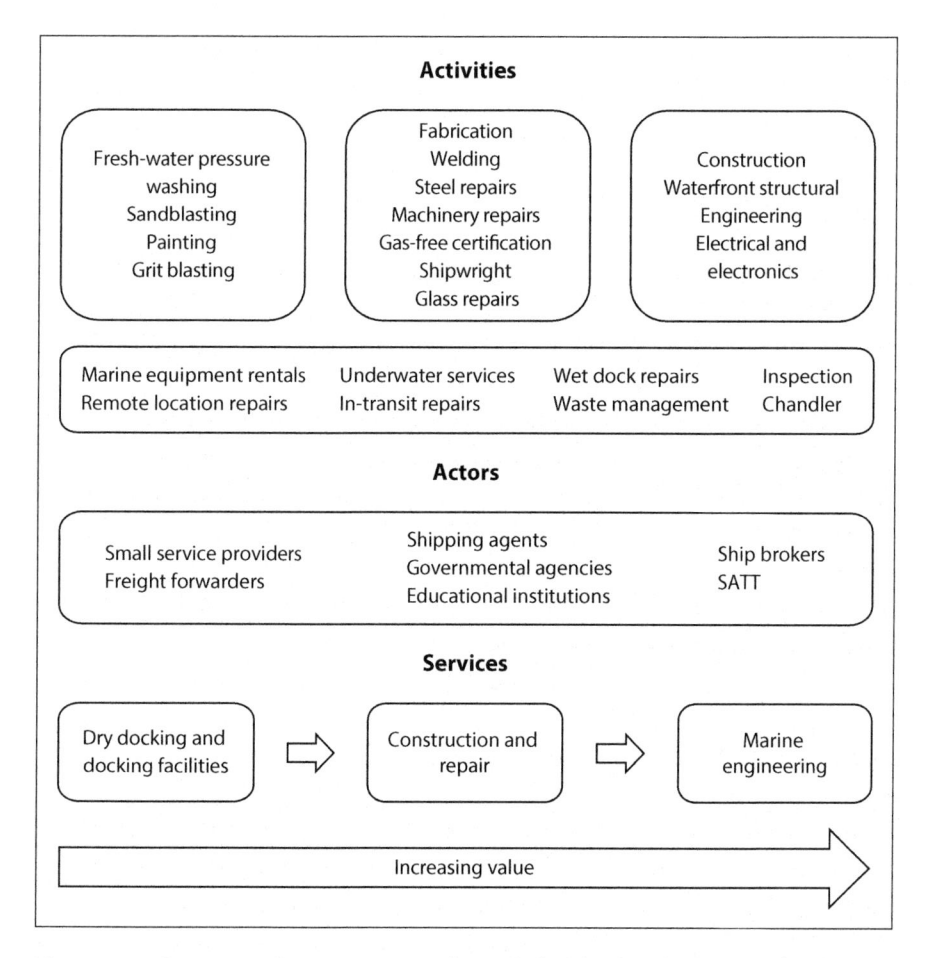

Figure 5.4. Overview of main activities of Trinidad and Tobago's ship repair industry

may then enter the GVC via the export of these specialized services regionally and internationally. This strategy could further assist Trinidad and Tobago with export diversification away from the hydrocarbon industry.

5.6 Local Competitiveness Factors

Trinidad and Tobago has a number of factors that favour the development of the ship repair cluster (figure 5.5). In order to meet the growing demand for ship repair services and to move up the ship repair value chain, there is a need to more effectively leverage the country's comparative advantages. These are discussed in the following sections, using Porter's Diamond of National Competitiveness.

5.6.1 Factor Conditions

Perhaps Trinidad and Tobago's location is its greatest competitive factor. It is situated below the hurricane belt in the Caribbean and has the sheltered waters of the Gulf of Paria that provide a site where ship repair can occur year-round, given favourable weather conditions.

The country's close proximity to North America, South America and the Panama Canal in Central America means it is ideally suited to attract vessels from north-south and south-south trade. In fact, the completion of the Panama Canal's expansion by 2016 is anticipated to result in an increase in both the amount and size of ships passing through the trade route. Trinidad and Tobago's close geographic location to the Panama Canal puts it in position to benefit from this increased transcontinental trade.

5.6.2 Demand Conditions

Trinidad and Tobago's hydrocarbon sector has been significant in stimulating demand for local ship repair and dry-docking services. This is because the hydrocarbon sector attracts marine vessels to the country for the purpose of exporting LNG, refined oil, Trinidad Lake Asphalt, ammonia, urea, methanol, steel billets and wire rods to markets in the Caribbean, the United States and Europe (de Gannes 2010). In addition, marine vessels provide offshore support for the hydrocarbon industry, especially in the deep waters of the Gulf of Paria and Atlantic Ocean around Trinidad and Tobago. This provides new business opportunities since vessels would need to be dry-docked to undertake some degree of ship repair and maintenance services in order to continue operating in these waters.

5.6.3 Related and Supporting Industries

Given the international scope of the industry, another competitiveness consideration is the importance of international industry, health and safety standards. Examples of the most significant certifications include ISO 9001-2000, Class certifications (Lloyds, DNV, BV, ABS, GL) and International Ship and Port Facility Security (ISPS) accreditation. Of these major players, only Caribbean Dockyard and Engineering Services Limited is ISO certified to Lloyds Registered 2008/9001 standards (www.ttdockyard.com).

5.6.4 Firm Strategy and Rivalry

Although there is the potential for increased business locally, the current structure of the ship repair industry (which is dominated by a few yards each with very specific capacities geared for specific types of vessels) has essentially removed the competitive element and replaced this with a culture of cooperation. There is room to leverage this culture of informal cooperation. The sharing of resources (tools, equipment, and labour) assists operators in their ability to provide services in the industry.

5.6.5 Role of Government

Due to the very small and segmented nature of the local ship repair industry, the role of government is essential in providing the necessary support to enable growth and movement up the value chain. One determinant of the competitiveness of a country's ship repair sector is the presence of technical-vocational and tertiary educational training. The University of the West Indies has degree programmes in various fields of engineering, and the University of Trinidad and Tobago offers degree programmes in maritime studies and engineering, which can help build labour competencies in the maritime field. Trinidad and Tobago's government has also attempted to expand tertiary education skill sets by subsidizing the cost of education via the Government Assistance for Tertiary Education programme. However, one local ship repair expert from Caribbean Dockyard and Engineering Services Limited interviewed in 2013 noted that courses and curriculum needed to be improved to produce graduates with the requisite practical training to support the cluster.

There are other competitive factors that are influenced directly by government policy. The corporate tax rate of 15 per cent on the chargeable profits for small companies operating in the marine industry is competitive when compared to regional and international competitors, with the exception of Bahrain and the Bahamas (0 per cent). Singapore has a corporate tax rate of 17 per cent,

China 25 per cent, Sri Lanka 28 per cent, Philippines 30 per cent, India 33.99 per cent and Japan 35.64 per cent (KPMG 2014). Regional competitors such as the United States have a corporate tax rate of 40 per cent, Brazil 34 per cent, Curaçao 27.5 per cent, Panama and Columbia 25 per cent (KPMG 2014). Import duty concessions are also extended to companies that have at least 50 per cent local ownership, at least five permanent employees and utilize locally produced raw materials (Discover TT website).

Finally, Trinidad and Tobago's trade policy includes a reciprocal multilateral trade agreement with the European Union. The country is in negotiation with Canada for the renewal of a bilateral trade agreement and has partial and bilateral agreements with Venezuela, Colombia, the Dominican Republic, Cuba and Costa Rica. Additionally, the country benefits from unilateral preferential trade with the United States as part of the Caribbean Basin Initiative. These initiatives are designed to allow smaller yards to build competencies and clientele in order to compete with peers locally and regionally. This objective will

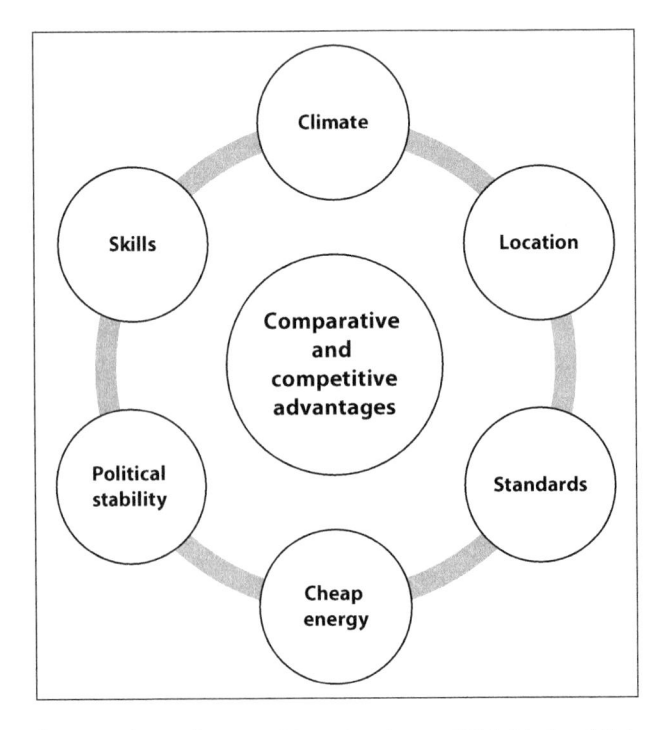

Figure 5.5. Comparative and competitive advantages of Trinidad and Tobago's ship repair industry

be especially important since the merchant marine sector, of which ship repair is a subset, has been targeted as one of the seven sectors for diversifying the economy (GORTT 2011, 2013).

5.6.6 Challenges for the Ship Repair Global Value Chain in Trinidad and Tobago

The Chaguaramas cluster has experienced a number of obstacles. According to a study by the Ministry of Trade, Industry, Investment and Communications, the ship repair industry faces difficulties in attracting and retaining competent and qualified personnel, especially in comparison to the higher paying energy sector (GORTT 2008). Additionally, there is need to expand the pool of mechanics, foremen, fabricators, divers, captains, draughtsmen, and health and safety personnel. Even when workers possess the requisite certificates, they often lack experience and require additional on-the-job training.

More training facilities are needed in order to ensure that workers are current with the latest technology. In order to do this, the Trinidad and Tobago government will have to decide whether they want to create a maritime tertiary education school or create new programmes at the University of the West Indies or the University of Trinidad and Tobago. The creation of new programmes may be cost effective; however, it will take a few years before graduates are released and can earn work experience.

New entrants in the industry may not have the track record required and can find it difficult to obtain financing. The industry's cost competitiveness is hampered by the fact that the majority of ship repair parts need to be imported and so will face import duties. There does not appear to be a comprehensive action plan for the industry. Some stakeholders from Interisle interviewed suggested this may be due to the lack of input in the consultation process by practitioners with industry-specific knowledge. These factors have contributed to there being few new start-up firms in the industry.

More targeted support from the government is needed to propel the expansion of the industry. Currently, there is an absence of tax concessions for ship repair companies. A favourable tax regime, especially for the import of repair parts, could act as a stimulus to this industry's growth. Government support is also desirable in strengthening trade with close regional partners, including CARICOM member states, as well as neighbouring countries in South America that could increase the volume of marine vessels entering Trinidad and Tobago's waters.

Another challenge is the declining US market for LNG exports. Recent improvement in hydraulic fracturing technology has led to increased shale gas production in the United States. There has subsequently been a decline in the US import of Trinidad and Tobago's LNG over the 2007 to 2013 period (www.eia.gov). Reduced LNG trade between Trinidad and Tobago and the United States would result in a reduction in LNG tankers from the United States, which could lead, in turn, to less demand for ship repair services in Trinidad and Tobago.

5.7 Lessons Learned

There are three main lessons emerging out of the GVC analysis of the Trinidad and Tobago ship repair industry.

1. Informal cooperation and networking arrangements have developed among the yards. Given the small pool of specialized labour which yards must access, they tend to "borrow" skilled personnel from each other. This strategy has been used to address periodic labour shortages when a yard lacks a specific labour skill set to complete a job.
2. Equipment "sharing" is a common practice. Tools and equipment required to perform certain jobs are often leased to competing firms. Thus, when a firm's work volume is reduced, or when its work does not require use of certain equipment, it may temporarily rent the equipment to another firm. Such strategic arrangements benefit both the owner and the renter of the equipment. The owner benefits from the additional cash flow when work is "slow", while the renter benefits from being able to access additional equipment.
3. Material is often shared within the cluster. Occasionally, a yard may lack all the materials to perform specific jobs. Given the close proximity of firms in the cluster, some of the firms have created informal arrangements where they may borrow raw material from a competitor, and replace or repurchase the material at a later date.

Although one may expect that aggressive competition among yards in the cluster must exist in order to facilitate upgrading and growth, these informal cooperative practices have provided some measure of stability and sustainability in the industry.

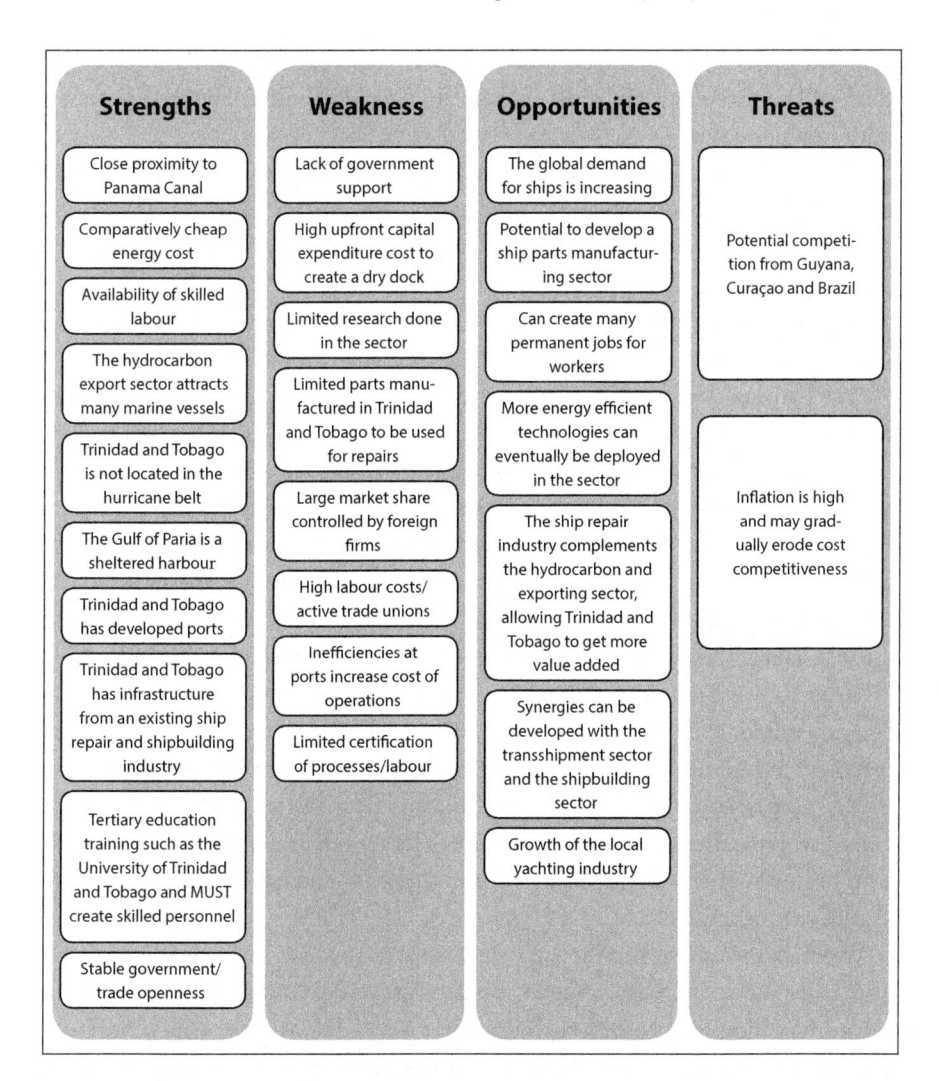

Strengths	Weakness	Opportunities	Threats
Close proximity to Panama Canal	Lack of government support	The global demand for ships is increasing	
Comparatively cheap energy cost	High upfront capital expenditure cost to create a dry dock	Potential to develop a ship parts manufacturing sector	Potential competition from Guyana, Curaçao and Brazil
Availability of skilled labour	Limited research done in the sector	Can create many permanent jobs for workers	
The hydrocarbon export sector attracts many marine vessels	Limited parts manufactured in Trinidad and Tobago to be used for repairs	More energy efficient technologies can eventually be deployed in the sector	
Trinidad and Tobago is not located in the hurricane belt	Large market share controlled by foreign firms	The ship repair industry complements the hydrocarbon and exporting sector, allowing Trinidad and Tobago to get more value added	Inflation is high and may gradually erode cost competitiveness
The Gulf of Paria is a sheltered harbour	High labour costs/ active trade unions		
Trinidad and Tobago has developed ports	Inefficiencies at ports increase cost of operations		
Trinidad and Tobago has infrastructure from an existing ship repair and shipbuilding industry	Limited certification of processes/labour	Synergies can be developed with the transshipment sector and the shipbuilding sector	
Tertiary education training such as the University of Trinidad and Tobago and MUST create skilled personnel		Growth of the local yachting industry	
Stable government/ trade openness			

Figure 5.6. SWOT analysis of Trinidad and Tobago's ship repair industry
Source: Authors' compilation.

5.8 Upgrading Strategies

Various upgrading strategies could be employed in order to grow the ship repair industry within Trinidad and Tobago. Upgrading occurs when firms or countries move into higher-value activities in GVCs in order to increase profits and employment. Government policy, firm strategy, technology and human capital can all lead to successful upgrading. In the GVC framework, four types of upgrading have been identified (Gereffi and Fernandez-Stark 2011). An explanation of the three that are most relevant to Trinidad and Tobago's ship repair value chain follows.

Process upgrading involves the transformation of inputs into outputs more efficiently or improvements to the efficiency of production. This can be done by reorganizing various activities in the ship repair cluster, adopting better technology and taking steps to create a more skilled labour force. Shipyards can undergo restructuring and streamline their operations to optimize resources in terms of manpower and facilities.

The University of the West Indies and the University of Trinidad and Tobago currently provide training in various technical and engineering fields. The University of the West Indies and the University of Trinidad and Tobago may need to increase their output of technical graduates in the ship repair industry. Furthermore, since young workers would be deficient in experience and may find difficulty in gaining employment, apprenticeship programmes are also needed. Such programmes should span at least two years with private sector firms in order to create the skill sets and on-the-job training required for this industry.

Research and continuous improvement in technology such as new hull designs, rudder and propeller design, LNG as fuel and ballast water management systems have allowed South Korea to emerge as a major player in the industry. Similar research at Trinidad and Tobago's universities to support technological improvements can help the country's ship repair companies to upgrade and become involved in the ship convergence and shipbuilding segment (Mickeviciene 2011).

Product upgrading for the maritime cluster involves serving larger ships. This will require increasing the number of grave-docks that are necessary for accommodating larger ships such as cruise liners. CL Marine, which has been acquired by the Trinidad and Tobago government, identified for upgrading and envisaged to be one of the largest dry-dock facilities in the world, has yet to materialize.

Trinidad and Tobago currently has companies operating in the ship repair, shipbuilding and marine engineering clusters. The government has signalled its interest in developing the yachting segment of the marine sector as a key activity in its economic diversification strategy (GORTT 2011, 2013). The increase in yachting activities presents a potential opportunity to both expand into a parallel marine sector and to expand the supply of vessels for maintenance services.

5.9 Recommendations

The ship repair industry has the potential to help Trinidad and Tobago's economy diversify. However, in order to facilitate the expansion and growth of the sector, a number of measures are needed.

5.9.1 Increasing the Supply of Skilled Labour

Training and certification in all technical areas needs to be increased. There is particular need for: welders, steel fabricators, pipe fitters, shipwrights, engineering technicians, confined space tank cleaners, blasters and painters, electricians and electronic technicians. Since the industry is governed by international classification societies such as Lloyds, the American Bureau of Shipping, the US Coast Guard and Bureau Veritas, training must meet these standards. The local universities – the University of Trinidad and Tobago and the University of the West Indies – can provide the technical training. Since the various international classification bodies have locally registered offices, they should work together with the local universities to ensure that the university graduates produce high-quality work that can meet the required standards. At the industry level, collaborations can help local firms improve marketing strategies and production. At the tertiary education level, training programmes can be designed to produce the high-quality graduates needed in the industry.

5.9.2 Partnerships with Local and International Technical Institutes

Many firms in the industry are unaware of their human resources requirements and have difficulty in attracting and retaining competent and qualified staff (Global Insights 2008). In order to address these deficiencies, maritime human resources training can be developed in Trinidad and Tobago's tertiary education institutions and training can be offered to firms in the industry. Partnerships can be established between tertiary intuitions and firms to perform human resources audits and help with training sessions.

5.9.3 Partnerships with International Yards

While local yards operating in the maritime industry are profitable in Trinidad and Tobago, it is unlikely that any of them will emerge as dominant world players. However, sustainability in this industry, or movement up the ship repair value chain may be possible through partnerships with international yards.

Collaborations in the form of mergers or acquisitions can be considered. If the multinational partner is vertically integrated, the smaller local partner may learn how to make upward transitions in the value chain towards shipbuilding and marine engineering.

The local partner may learn the logistics required to manage multiple segments of the value chain in order to capture greater value added. For example, a local firm may build a marine vessel for a client, but it may also offer the client, ship repair services at a discount for a period of time.

The mergers would also be necessary for upgrading technical staff. For instance, the local partner may send local workers to the shipyard of the multinational partner for training, and the multinational partner may periodically send some of their specialized workers to offer skills and train local technical staff. Since the ship repair industry uses specialized equipment, improvements, technologies and processes can also be introduced to the local partner. Such collaborations could improve the productivity of labour, the efficiency of local firms and the management skill of the local partner. This could also lead to an expansion in the range of services the local ship repair partner can offer and an increase in the volume of work undertaken by the local ship repair company. Improved logistics and efficiency can result in decreases in per unit costs, and subsequently increase the profitability of local ship repair firms.

5.9.4 Greater Cooperation among Stakeholders

In order for Trinidad and Tobago to fully capitalize on the benefits of the maritime sector, it needs to increase local content by expanding local ownership and encouraging local entrepreneurs to enter the industry. As previously mentioned, the ship repair cluster performs a range of services that includes: welding, machinery repair, painting and maintenance and electrical repairs. Potential entrepreneurs should therefore attempt to target niches in the cluster, many of which can be serviced by sole traders and small businesses. Targeting niches in the cluster would also create employment and earn revenue for local businesses.

Stronger collaboration is needed between stakeholders in the industry. The Ministry of Trade, Industry, Investment and Communication in collaboration with business and technical institutions can offer programmes to improve specific areas of company operations that may inhibit growth.

Greater interministerial coordination would reduce bureaucracy, especially at ports, and this would improve the efficiency of importing tools, parts and equipment.

5.9.5 Protect Liquefied Natural Gas Export Markets

As previously indicated, Trinidad and Tobago's ship repair industry thrives on work from the energy industry. However, the shale oil and gas boom in the United States has altered the economic dynamics of energy as the United States gradually becomes energy independent and may become a LNG exporter post-2015. Trinidad and Tobago has adjusted to this dynamic by diversifying its LNG export base, with approximately 60 per cent of its LNG exports going the Latin American market (British Petroleum 2015). Some spot cargos from the United States may enter the Latin American market post-2015 and erode Trinidad and Tobago's market share.

In 2014, Chilean ambassador Fernando Schmidt, publicly lobbied Trinidad and Tobago to consider engaging in discussions with Chile for a Partial Scope Trade Agreement in natural gas (John-Lall 2014). This policy was proposed as a means to strengthen trade relations between Chile and Trinidad and Tobago, and lock in natural gas supplies from Trinidad and Tobago.

If Trinidad and Tobago utilizes a bilateral Partial Scope Trade Agreement in natural gas with its trading partners in the Latin American region, it would secure its market share from potential US competition post-2015. Furthermore, strengthening the trade relations between regional partners could increase the volume of marine trade in Trinidad and Tobago. This increase in volume could result in increased ship repair work as some vessels would require maintenance.

5.9.6 Enabling Environment

For several reasons, financing may be a challenge for many new and small firms entering the ship repair cluster. In the case of new entrants, financial institutions are unwilling to provide loans to firms that have no proven track record in the industry as these are deemed "high risk". This tends to be a serious disincentive to new entrants. Firms which have been operating for some time in the industry have also listed financing as a key challenge, mainly because of the high interest rates which accompany loans in the maritime industry (interviews with staff of Interisle, 2013).

In order to address this, the Trinidad and Tobago government can follow Brazil's maritime policy and establish a fund geared towards financing of local ship repair businesses. Low-interest loans can be offered to firms that meet certain credit requirements. This financing would result in an increase in new or start-up firms in the industry. If such financing is provided in addition to the outreach programme from the Ministry of Trade, Industry, Investment and Communication, the government can directly guide entrepreneurs and small businesses as they transition into larger and more resilient enterprises. These policy recommendations would directly lead to increases in employment, and may lead to the lateral and vertical expansion of firms in the ship repair value chain.

Another government strategy could be the provision of tax concessions for new businesses for a fixed period. Import tax concessions can also be deployed on imported ship repair parts in the short run. These would provide new and small businesses with a cost advantage to assist them in competing in the local industry.

In the long run, since parts manufacturing represents another candidate cluster for diversification, the government could seek to attract foreign investment to establish manufacturing activities in the cluster. If this is established, it will create jobs, earn foreign exchange, build labour skill sets, and increase output in the economy of Trinidad and Tobago via the multiplier effect. The new cluster could also increase the amount of taxation revenue collected by the Trinidad and Tobago government as there would be more business activity to tax. Competitive advance factors such as the existence of an iron and steel industry, cheap electricity, a skilled labour base, extensive roads and public utilities infrastructure, and a ship repair cluster that would demand such parts makes the potential parts manufacturing cluster more feasible.

The government could also play a lead role by strengthening ties and trade with other countries. Trinidad and Tobago's recent strengthening of trade relations with China can be used to its advantage – China is a global player in the ship repair and shipbuilding industry and has many firms that could form joint ventures with Trinidad and Tobago companies, thereby creating positive spillover effects. These joint ventures may allow local firms to horizontally and vertically diversify their operations. The increased business activity could increase employment opportunities and taxation collection for the government. Increased trade with China would also result in a greater number of marine vessels needing repair.

Government effort is also needed for the improvement of the marketing of the ship repair and transshipment sector. Based on Trinidad and Tobago's location, potential trade lanes to focus on include: Panama/South American east coast (high priority), South American east coast/US gulf coast (medium priority), southern Europe/Panama (medium priority), and South American east coast/southeast United States (low priority).

5.10 Conclusion

The foregoing analysis suggests that there is potential for the expansion of the Chaguaramas ship repair cluster and for replication of this cluster in other targeted ports. Expansion and competitive activities within this sector will depend on active public–private sector participation in which both identify strengths, weaknesses and opportunities at the global, regional and industry and firm levels and develop strategic plans to build on the country's competitive strengths. This will involve targeted policies to increase the quantity and quality of industry-relevant skills and the incentives and infrastructural framework for the industry. Labour costs, attitudes towards work, inconsistency in costs and delivery have eroded the cluster's competitive edge vis-à-vis regional competitors and must therefore be factored into firms' strategies. It is anticipated that expansion of the Chaguaramas ship repair cluster will entail not only an increase in the number of repairs and related activities annually, but also a move along the value chain through the increase in more specialized activities and the export of specialized marine services regionally and internationally.

Notes

1. South Korea, Japan and China have yards dedicated solely to ship repair.
2. This was assuming an exchange rate between Trinidad and Tobago and the United States as TT$6.40 = US$1.00.

References

British Petroleum. 2015. "Statistical Review of World Energy".
Caribbean Maritime. 2012. "Curaçao Sees Growth". Issue 16: Ports and Terminals, 25–26. https://issuu.com/landmarine/docs/cm16.
Central Bank of Trinidad and Tobago. 2013. *Annual Economic Survey.* http://www.central-bank.org.tt/sites/default/files/AES%20Report%202013_Online%20Version.pdf.
CESA (Community of European Shipyards' Association). 2011. *Annual Report 2010–2011.* Brussels: CESA. http://forumokretowe.org.pl/files/news_pl_19.pdf.
CSO (Central Statistical Office of Trinidad and Tobago). 2013. "Gross Domestic Product Data 2009–2013".
de Gannes, W. 2010. "Strategic Plan for Trinidad and Tobago's Ship Repair and Ship Building Industry for the Period 2011–2012". Shipbuilding and Repair Development Company of Trinidad and Tobago Ltd. http://issuu.com/shipbuildingandrepairdocuments.
de Gannes, W., and A. Persad. 2010. "Development of Shipbuilding and Ship Repair Industry in Trinidad and Tobago". IEM 2010, Conference of Fostering Engineering Networking, Collaboration and Competence, Trinidad and Tobago.
Gereffi, G., and K. Fernandez-Stark. 2011. *Global Value Chain Analysis: A Primer.* Durham, NC: Duke University Center on Globalization, Governance and Competitiveness. http://www.cggc.duke.edu/pdfs/2011-05-31_GVC_analysis_a_primer.pdf.
Global Insights. 2008. "Consultancy Services for the Domestic Maritime Industry in the Development of Business Plans for Key Maritime Clusters". Final report.
GORTT (Government of the Republic of Trinidad and Tobago). 2008. Ministry of Trade, Industry, Investment and Communications. "Maritime Sector". http://www.tradeind.gov.tt/Portals/0/Documents/Brief%20on%20the%20Maritime%20Industry%20%20for%20Website-%20May%202013.pdf.
———. 2011. "Medium Term Policy Framework, 2011–2014". http://finance.gov.tt/wp-content/uploads/2013/11//Medium-Term-Policy-Framework-2011-14.pdf.
———. 2013. Ministry of Trade, Industry, Investment and Communications. "Seven Sectors Earmarked for Development". http://www.ttmissionsnigeria.com/trade/SevenSectors.pdf.
InvesTT. 2012. *A Guide to Investing in Trinidad and Tobago.* http://www.investt.co.tt/publications/investt-guide-to-investing-in-tt.pdf.
John-Lall, R. 2014. "Ambassador: Trinidad and Tobago Exports US$1bn in Products to Chile". *Trinidad and Tobago Guardian*, 18 September.
KPMG. 2014. *Corporate and Indirect Tax Rate Survey.* http://www.kpmg.com/Global/en/IssuesAndInsights/ArticlesPublications/Documents/corporate-indirect-tax-rate-survey-2014.pdf.

Mickeviciene, R. 2011. "Global Competition in Shipbuilding: Trends and Challenges for Europe". *Economic Geography of Globalization*. http://gendocs.ru/docs/38/37028/conv_1/file1.pdf#page=213.

OECD (Organisation for Economic Co-operation and Development). 2008. "The Interaction between the Ship Repair, Ship Conversion and Ship Building Industries". http://www.oecd.org/sti/ind/42033278.pdf.

World Bank. 2014. *World Development Indicators 2014*. Washington, DC: World Bank.

CASE STUDY 6

The Future of Solar Water Heaters in Barbados
Market Expansion or Product Innovation?

ANDREA N. BALDWIN
Assistant Professor
Connecticut College

OLIVIA CHASE-SMITH
Consultant
Performance Pro Business Solutions

Abstract

Solar water heating (SWH) is an example of early pioneering manufacturing and the sustainable application of renewable energy technology in Barbados. According to the International Energy Agency, Barbados is among leading countries in the world in SWH water collector capacity, ranking fourth behind Cyprus, Israel and Austria. The country dominates the Caribbean regional export market for SWH systems, accounting for approximately 80 per cent of the demand.

Despite these figures, manufacturers of solar water heaters (SWHs) in Barbados have yet to penetrate markets outside of the Caribbean and compete on a global scale. To boost growth, these firms must decide if they should upgrade their existing SWH products to include new value-added solar technologies. Additionally, they need to consider how they can improve domestic and regional market penetration while also attempting to engage customers outside the Caribbean.

This report examines the SWH industry in Barbados and documents the successes, challenges and barriers to export growth and competitiveness. Based on the research, several recommendations are offered to assist the industry's development. These include upgrades to the product through newer solar technologies, upgrades within the SWH value chain, inducements towards a greater domestic appetite for solar and renewable energy products, and adjustments to the sector's domestic fiscal and regulatory policy regime.

6.1 Introduction

Like many small island developing states in the Caribbean, Barbados relies heavily on imported fossil fuels, which provides 95 per cent of the country's energy (Bugler 2012). In an effort to reduce its dependence on foreign oil, Barbados's government first tried to nurture the development of the SWH industry in the early 1970s through strategies such as the Fiscal Incentives Act of 1974, which provided tax breaks on raw materials to SWH manufacturers. The government's assistance resulted in the formation of the first SWH company on the island in the same year. Later legislation which proved vital to the industry's growth included the following: a tax benefit that allowed homeowners to claim the cost of SWHs against income taxes, mandates to install SWHs on new government housing developments (Headley 2001), and higher tax rates for non-solar units (Bugler 2012). Today, SWHs are standard features in the construction of new houses, and Barbados accounts for the use of over 55 per cent of the SWHs in the region and the manufacture of 80 per cent (Gardner 2011).

Despite the early success of the SWH industry in Barbados, business has stagnated in recent years. The industry's sluggishness can be attributed to the maturity of the sector, high retail prices and the absence of an updated government strategy to replace initial efforts in the 1970s and 1980s. However, the recent increase of global interest in the solar industry could lead to a revival of the SWH sector in Barbados if appropriate strategies are implemented.

This study attempts to assess the competitiveness of the SWH industry in Barbados and whether it can be considered a successful renewable energy sector. It also highlights lessons and best practices that can be used to propel the development of the broader nascent renewable energy sector in Barbados. It is concerned with answering the following questions:

1. Should SWH manufacturers in Barbados upgrade their existing products to incorporate other solar technologies such as photovoltaic systems (PV)?
2. Should SWH manufacturers in Barbados diversify their product offering to domestic, regional and global markets?
3. Given Barbados's small size and limited financial and human resources, how feasible are these strategies?

This study examines the SWH industry in Barbados using global value chain (GVC) methodology and data gathered from interviews with industry stakeholders such as SunPower Limited – a major company in Barbados that assembles, sizes, installs and services SWHs for both residential and commercial use.

Using this information, the study maps the progress of the industry and highlights its experiences and successes, concentrating on those related to the export of products outside of the region. It assesses the industry's competitive environment, capabilities and strategies and then concludes by making projections and recommendations on how to improve the industry's success abroad.

6.2 The Solar Water Heating System and the Global Value Chain

The production and distribution of SWH units which is illustrated by the SWH global value chain, consists of six stages (see figure 6.1). These stages include raw materials, components, the manufacture of the finished product, sales and distribution of the product, installation, and post-sales services. Each stage of the value chain is dominated by a few major global players, but those who manufacture the SWHs are also usually involved in the installation process.

6.2.1 Solar Water Heater Production

Water is heated when a SWH system absorbs solar energy through its thermal collector. SWH systems are available in many configurations and are used in multiple applications to provide water-heating solutions to residential, commercial and industrial customers (Navigant 2010). There are two types of SWHs: (1) active, which have circulating pumps and controls, and (2) passive, which do not. Passive SWH systems are typically less expensive than active systems, but they are typically not as efficient.[1] Most SWHs require a well-insulated storage tank, and this tank has to be connected to the collector. There are three types of solar collectors that are used for residential applications: flat-plate collectors,[2] integral collector-storage systems, and the evacuated-tube solar collectors.[3]

6.3 Solar Water Heaters: A Global Perspective

In contrast to many other renewable energy technologies, the majority of firms in SWH are large companies from the broader heating and thermal sector or independent actors. These businesses remain highly fragmented, with only one in four global companies producing more than thirty-five megawatts per year, and the largest group manufacturing fewer than seven megawatts (REN21 2012). In 2010, the industry consisted of two hundred manufacturers and

MATERIALS	COMPONENTS	MANUFACTURE OF FINISHED PRODUCT	SALES AND DISTRIBUTION	INSTALLATION	POST-SALES SERVICE
Steel	Storage tanks	Fabrication	Local	Measuring	Repairs
Copper	Heat exchanger	Assembly	Regional	Mounting	Service
Bauxite	Electronic controls	Inspection	International	Fastening	Warranty
Glass	Fractional pumps	Commission		Caulking	
Zinc	Pump motor			Sealing	
Plastic	Hydronic valves			Wiring	
	Expansion tank				
	Air elimination valve				
	Piping and fittings				
	Temperature gauge				
	Pressure gauge				
	Drain back tank				
	Glass fibre				
	Thermostat				
	Insulation				
	Polyurethane				

Education and training

Research and development

Policies and regulations

Figure 6.1. Solar water heater global value chain

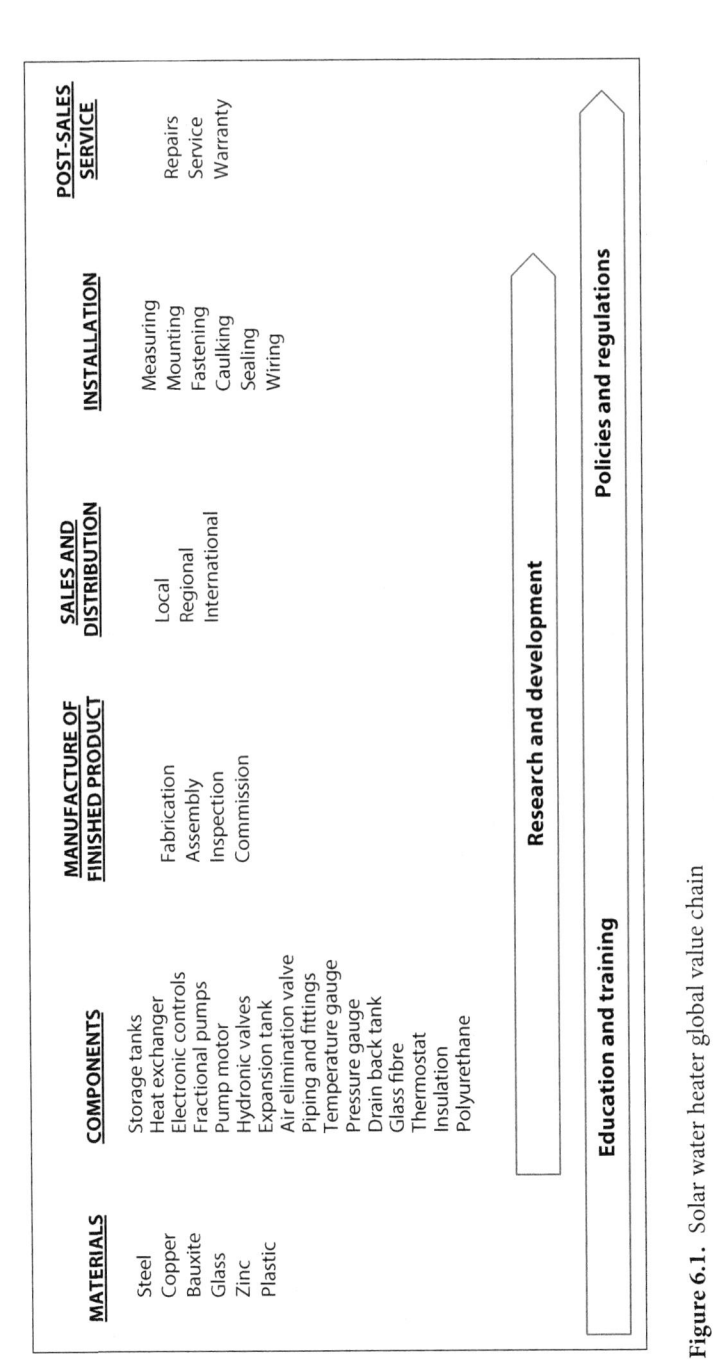

approximately one thousand installers globally (REN21 2012). The largest firms are starting to integrate vertically to cover all stages of manufacturing.

China has been steadily gaining market share in the SWH sector. Indeed, China led the world in solar thermal glazed installations in 2011, accounting for an estimated 58 per cent of global capacity, with Europe a distant second. While most Chinese production is installed domestically, its export of solar thermal products has also increased considerably in recent years (REN21 2012). In 2007, China's exports of SWHs grew by 28 per cent to US$65 million, driven largely by the exports of companies such as Linuo New Materials, Sangle, Micoe, Himin, the Sunrain Group Jiangsu and Beijing Tsinghua Solar. While Chinese firms export to approximately fifty countries and territories in Europe, the United States and Southeast Asia, an important share of exports is demanded by developing countries in Africa and Central and South America, where warmer climates support the use of thermosyphon systems.[4] To support their entry into the emerging South American market (REN21 2012), several firms have established manufacturing operations in Jamaica (interview with Henry Jordan, 5 June 2013). However, it must be noted that Chinese firms' ability to produce SWHs and lead the industry is partly based on government subsidies. This subsidization could be potentially damaging to Barbados's industry, as worldwide solar companies have the capacity to manufacture between sixty and seventy gigawatts' worth of solar panels a year, well above expected global demand (Bullis 2013).

Europe remains a key player in the industry both in terms of demand and supply. In recent years, the European sector has been marked by mergers and acquisitions, especially among lead firms in Germany, which accounted for almost half of the flat-plate producers in 2007 but only made up one-third in 2012. Additionally, new facilities within Europe have come online to meet rising demand in Brazil, India, Turkey and elsewhere, particularly in the developing south (REN21 2012). These developing country SWH export markets are expanding rapidly, in part because of programmes such as *Minha Casa, Minha Vida* (My House, My Life) in Brazil, which mandates SWHs in local low-income housing and accounts for 20 per cent of 2011 sales (REN21 2012).

6.3.1 Global Standards

SWHs are typically known for high initial investment, followed by low operating costs and a lifespan of fifteen to twenty years depending upon the type of solar collector. Considering these factors, maintaining high quality in manufacturing is essential to delivering uninterrupted services over the life cycle of the technology. As such, the International Organization for Standardization and its members regularly develop and revise product standards for SWHs. These include the latest revisions to ISO 9459, which governs system performance through whole-system tests and computer simulations.

There also have been efforts to make SWH product standards applicable at the country and regional level. In 2003, European manufacturers developed the Keymark voluntary certification scheme with the support of the European Solar Thermal Industry Federation. This label is recognized in most European countries and facilitates the movement of products between European Union member states by making it easier for SWH producers to gain direct access to financial incentives such as subsidies and loans, without the need for compliance with specific national standards (Menanteau 2007). It is also used by the Chinese government to develop its own national technical standards for solar thermal equipment. China's aim is to gain easier access to the European market for its solar products and to develop technical standards in China.

In addition to standards, special contractual approaches have also been developed with the goal of guaranteeing or improving the quality of SWH systems. For example, the Guarantee of Solar Results project has been implemented on an experimental basis in certain countries such as France and Spain. Applicable to large installations, its aim is to check that the real performance of a system corresponds to advertised performance and to compensate users if this is not the case (Menanteau 2007).

6.3.2 Solar Energy Agreements and Cooperation Frameworks

The World Trade Organization has expressed its support for trade agreements to facilitate the development of green economies across the globe. In February 2013, the European Union and the United States announced plans to begin negotiating a broad transatlantic free-trade agreement to develop partnerships with regard to the development of renewable energy technologies and trade in renewables.

However, trade disputes between the European Union, United States and China are likely to derail any efforts for the development of global trade agreements in solar energy, at least in the short term. In August 2013, the European Union and China settled a trade conflict after the European Union allowed approximately "100 Chinese companies to export tariff-free to the EU, as long as they keep their prices above fifty-six European cents (seventy-six US cents) per watt of solar-panel generation". The threshold has since been lowered slightly, but European solar panel manufacturers still have concerns about potential violations to the settlement (Dalton 2014).

While Europe is China's principal market for solar panels, accounting for 80 per cent of exports ("EU-Chinese Trade", *Economist*, 18 June 2013), China and the United States have also had similar disputes. In June 2014, the US Commerce Department imposed duties of 19–35 per cent on Chinese solar panel manufacturers after ruling that they had benefited from unfair government subsidies. In July 2014, the Department of Commerce then found that Chinese solar companies had dumped solar products on the American market at below cost and imposed duties of 7 per cent to 55.5 per cent (Cardwell and Bradsher 2014).

Combined, the strong position of European and Chinese exporters, global agreements and standards makes it difficult for other manufacturers to compete in the export market. Conforming to certifications and competing against European and Chinese firms can prove to be cost prohibitive, especially when factored into the already high costs of producing global-quality SWHs.

6.4 Overview of the Local Solar Water Heating Industry in Barbados

The SWH industry in Barbados received early assistance from the Barbados government in the early 1970s (interview with William Hinds, 30 May 2013). Since then the industry has adopted a very insular characteristic with little cooperation among the several small and medium-sized companies.

6.4.1 Actors in the Barbados Value Chain

Market share is divided among five leading small and medium-sized enterprises. In recent years, market share among the key players has remained relatively unchanged (Jordan interview, 2013). Although the number of major firms in the SWH sector is stable, there are more companies providing solar energy solutions and associated PV services in the market. Table 6.1 summarizes the profile of the five leading firms in the Barbados's SWH industry.

Table 6.1. Domestic Firms in the Solar Water Heating Sector in Barbados

Industry Players	Year Established and Country of Ownership	Product (P) and Services (S)	Number of Employees	Present Market Share (Based on Unit Sales)	Growth in Market Share 1970–2012	Export Markets
SunPower	1978 Barbados	P: Flat-panel collector S: Repairs on all brands of solar water heater Customer financing After-hours emergency assistance	Management: 9 Office: 9 Service: 28	Approximately 35 per cent	Undetermined	Barbados Antigua Grenada St Vincent
Solar Dynamics	1974 Barbados	P: Natural circulation/convection Split circulation installations (pumped) S: 89 per cent of tanks can be repaired Free loaner tank while tank is being repaired		Approximately 40 per cent	Undetermined	Anguilla Antigua and Barbuda Bahamas Belize Dominica Grenada Guyana Montserrat Nevis Suriname St Kitts St Lucia St Maarten St Vincent and Grenadines Tortola

AquaSol	1981 Barbados	S: Customer financing	Company bought by Solaris in 2010
Solaris	2010 Trinidad and Tobago		N/a
Solar Apex	2008 Barbados	P: Flat panel collector S: Installation Customer consultation Colour-coding of systems Repairs and maintenance to other brands Special financing arrangements for customer payments	N/a

Source: Authors, based on interviews with key firms.

6.5 Support for the Solar Water Heating Industry

6.5.1 Government Support

Beginning in the 1970s, the SWH industry in Barbados enjoyed tremendous support from the government and experienced positive growth. Assistance included fiscal measures intended to spur growth in the industry such as tax incentives for residential and commercial consumers. Successive governments continued to introduce policies to support the SWH industry. Noting the prevalence of SWH installations on the island (50,000 SWH units for Barbados's 200,000 residents), some researchers have concluded that the government's initiatives were instrumental in boosting the SWH industry (Bugler 2012). Table 6.2 shows the chronology of fiscal incentives provided to the SWH sector.

With regards to energy consumption, the Barbados government projects that the energy mix for the country will be 70 per cent natural, 20 per cent petroleum and 10 per cent other fossil fuel by 2026 (Hinds interview, 2013). The business sector and households alike are now more educated to the cost benefits

Table 6.2. Fiscal Incentives to Stimulate the Solar Water Heating Sector in Barbados

1974
Fiscal Incentives Act

1977
Government purchase of solar water heaters for state housing

1980–1992
Homeowner Tax Benefit

1996
Homeowner Tax Benefit (amended)

2006
Conditional exemptions for energy conservation by waiving the import duty on energy systems

2008
Energy conservation and renewable energy deduction of a maximum of $5,000 per year over each of five years to cover the costs of an energy audit; and 50 per cent of the cost of retrofitting a residence or installing a system to produce electricity from a source other than fossil fuels.

2011
Increase in income tax deduction for individuals and businesses

of alternative solar energy solutions such as SWH. However, fuel subsidies continue to distort prices, encouraging inefficient consumption and dependence on traditional energy sources.

6.5.2 Research and Technical Support

The design of SWHs has remained relatively unchanged in the last thirty years, and flat-plate collectors continue to dominate the Barbados market. Stakeholders in the sector are making efforts to develop new products – the Fair Trading Commission, for instance, is engaged in discussions on storage of excess energy produced by residential and commercial users (interview with representative of the Barbados Fair Trading Commission, 2013). Independent entrepreneurs and innovators in the domestic market have also immersed themselves in creative solar energy activities ranging from solar ovens to power ice-makers in fishing vessels and cooling and air-conditioning systems (interview with Tom Rogers, 11 June 2013).

Despite these efforts, the Centre for Resource Management and Environmental Studies at the University of the West Indies reports that not enough research and development is taking place and that it is unlikely that Barbados will lead innovation efforts given the significant research and commercial applications already done by sector leaders such as Germany and China (ibid.). What is currently being investigated and might ultimately hold more potential, is research into applications that are specific to Caribbean needs such as solar cooling systems and solar drying facilities for use in agriculture. Evolution of the sector is expected to be driven by the private sector, where research will respond to the requirements of private enterprises (Hinds interview, 2013). It is possible that strategic partnerships among researchers, private enterprises and innovators will have a critical role in any future success of the industry (interview with Mark Hill, 31 May 2013).

6.6 Local Industry Conditions

While incentives and a greater understanding of the benefits of SWH have helped to drive growth in the sector, the domestic industry in Barbados appears to have lost some of its momentum. Today, it is increasingly characterized by sluggish growth, stagnant market share, high prices and low levels of innovation.

6.6.1 Demand Conditions

Domestic growth prospects appear weak. Close to 90 per cent of larger homes already have SWHs installed (Barbados Light and Power Holdings 2012), while smaller homes in the country often lack the financial resources to purchase these systems, which cost an average of US$2,000 each. The high cost of SWH units is a defining characteristic of the local industry. A SWH unit in China costs less than US$200; in Barbados, a similar product costs roughly ten times that amount (Gardner 2011). However, using fiscal incentives as a way to mitigate the cost difference is likely to be ineffective since many of these households are already exempt from income tax.[5]

In addition to the maturing domestic SWH market, the global recession has also contributed to the decline in the domestic market share for new purchases of SWHs in the residential and commercial markets. In the prevailing environment, sales are being driven by customer referrals. In an attempt to reach new clients, manufacturers have developed strategies aimed at making SWH units more accessible to consumers. New marketing packages include offering instalment-type financing arrangements as well as partnering with retail distributors (who have a wider consumer base) to offer similar lease-sales

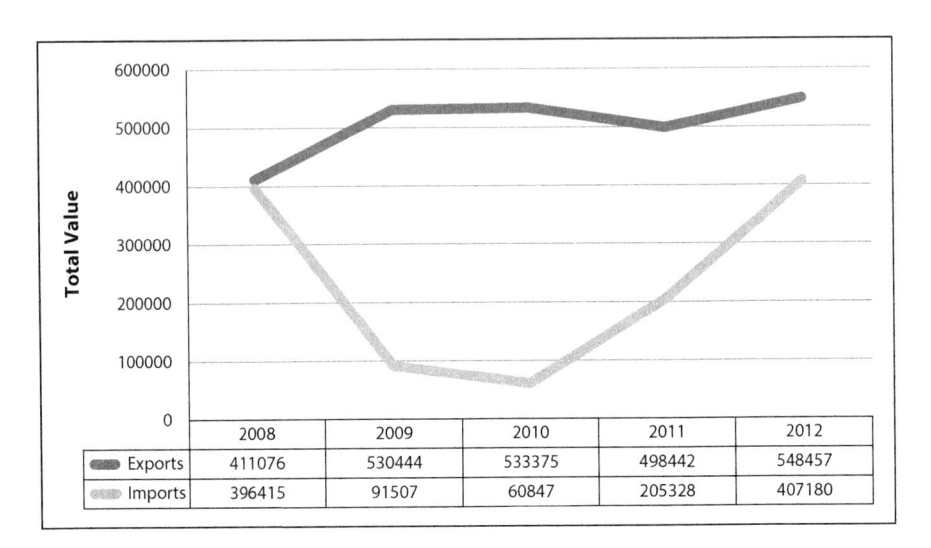

	2008	2009	2010	2011	2012
Exports	411076	530444	533375	498442	548457
Imports	396415	91507	60847	205328	407180

Figure 6.2. Imports and exports of solar water heaters in Barbados, 2008–2012
Source: Barbados Statistical Service.

agreements (Jordan interview, 2013). Figure 6.2 shows relatively stable export performance during the period 2008–2012.

6.7 Factor Conditions

6.7.1 Standards and Certification

As solar and renewable energy have assumed greater importance, countries in the region are also establishing priorities for standards development (interview with Fabien Scott, 3 June 2013; interview with Felix St Prix, 4 June 2013).

Table 6.3. Barbados National Standards Applied to Solar Water Heaters and Renewable Energy

Barbados National Standard Code	Name	Details
BNS 147: 1983	Barbados National Standard specification for method of thermal testing of flat-plate solar collectors	Describes outdoor tests for determining the thermal performance of flat-plate solar collectors using water as a fluid and natural radiation from the sun.
International Electro-technical Commission	Salt mist corrosion testing of photovoltaic modules	Tests the deterioration or corrosion of module components from salt mist.
International Standard	Ultraviolet test for photovoltaic modules	A test which determines the resistance of the module when exposed to ultra-violet radiation – materials such as polymers and protective coatings.
International Standard – IEC 61853-1	Photovoltaic module performance testing and energy rating	A guide to mapping module performance over a wide range of temperature and irradiance conditions – methods for characterizing spectral and angular effects; definition of reference climatic profiles; methods for evaluating instantaneous power and energy results; and a method for stating these results in the form of a numerical rating.

Source: Barbados National Standards Institute.

Industry standards have evolved from prescriptive standards to performance-based standards. The standards applied to the Barbados industry are voluntary standards stipulated by the World Trade Organization. Table 6.3 highlights the individual standards applied in Barbados:

6.8 Firm Strategies

6.8.1 Competitiveness Strategies

The SWH industry currently competes on price and customer value-added strategies (interview with Paul Pounder, 28 June 2013). Price differences can often be explained by differences in the quality of the product's components, its durability and its heat retention capacity. Over the years, companies have also assumed responsibility for servicing competitors' products. In addition, market hedging (securing future prices at present-day rates) for component inputs has become essential to the industry's survival and abates the potential negative impact of market price increases for the same component parts necessary for the manufacture of SWHs (Jordan interview, 2013).

6.9 Lessons Learned

Having applied the GVC methodology, four main lessons emerge about the SWH industry in Barbados:

6.9.1 Government Incentives Do Not Correlate to Industry Efficiency

This case provides evidence that government incentives sometimes lead to market failure. In its nascent stages, domestic government policies generated important growth in the sector and incentivized consumer investment in the purchase and use of SWH technology. However, these policies did not sufficiently encourage manufacturers to pursue cost-efficiencies (such as passing competitive prices on to consumers) or long-term sustainability of the industry. Rather, government incentives created a form of protectionism for the sector.

6.9.2 Lack of Innovation, Research and Technology Development Suffocate Industry Growth

Little or no innovation, investment in research or technology in an industry or sector is positively correlated to its stagnation and obsolescence. Although the industry collectively made improvements to the apparatus of the SWH system, the net effect was insufficient innovation over the industry lifespan. Global research and development suggests that more could have been done to develop the domestic sector. However, the industry maintained the high prices of SWH units, antiquated features of some of the products in comparison to global products, and a lack of industry cooperation.

Market research and innovation are critical for the future of the sector, but are lacking in Barbados. The broader renewable energy sector has since evolved and introduced new technology such as PV energy solutions.

6.9.3 Lack of Inter- and Intra-industry Cooperation Impedes Industry Development

Due to its insularity, the sector has been negatively affected by its failure to capitalize on collective synergies and key stakeholder partnerships with agencies such as the Centre for Resource Management and Environmental Studies and international funding agencies. These types of partnerships could have facilitated important research and development funded by the University of the West Indies, while implementation of the research findings would be conducted by industry players.

6.9.4 Gaunt Cultural Appetite for Renewable Energy Products Inhibits Industry Growth

There appears to be a gaunt domestic appetite for renewable energy products – perhaps due to a lack of knowledge about the associated financial, environmental and economic benefits – and this has contributed to stunted industry growth. If consumers are not informed about a product, service or industry, then market demand will be affected since businesses will be attempting to solve a market problem or meet a market demand which does not exist due to lack of market information.

6.10 Recommended Strategies

This section outlines a number of recommendations which could potentially improve the competitive prospects and profitability of the SWH industry in Barbados (see table 6.4)

6.10.1 Innovation: Horizontal Integration and Product Upgrading

In GVC literature, product upgrading refers to improvements in the quality and sophistication of goods or services produced (Gereffi and Fernandez-Stark 2011). With the entire region increasing policy initiatives to make hot water and solar electricity available to rural populations, this could translate into opportunity and demand for partnerships to provide, install, and service SWHs (Martinot 2012). The industry in Barbados might benefit from entering into strategic intra-industry partnerships that focus on product developments which match local needs and expectations. These design modifications should extend beyond Barbadian consumers so that the product is more appealing for export to culturally diverse markets. Commensurate with product improvement should be investment in manufacturing materials which maintain affordability to the consumer – these combined initiatives would both reduce manufacturing costs within the value chain and increase profitability.

6.10.2 Chain Upgrading: Photovoltaic Production

Chain upgrading involves firms using their products in new ways to enter different industries or sectors. A value chain activity related to the SWH GVC involves the PV sector. The SWH industry in Barbados may be able to translate the knowledge it has developed in SWH technologies into the PV sector and also take advantage of the skills training and educational programmes made available by the Barbados government to develop the workforce necessary to improve the sector. In addition, the industry is well poised to capitalize on its brand recognition to enter the regional market for PV production and installation. There is also potential to partner with other developing markets in South America to gain global experience and engage in knowledge transfer. Partnering

Table 6.4. Upgrading Strategies, Potential Barriers and Business Model Proposals for the Solar Water Heating Industry in Barbados

Strategy	Steps	Barriers to Upgrading	Characteristics of a Successful Solar Water Heating Business Model
Horizontal integration	Partner with other solar water heating firms (local regional and extra regional) to expand current production so as to meet a larger Caribbean and extra-Caribbean demand and to move toward inter-chain upgrading	• Lack of transport • Lack of skilled work force • High costs • Market regulations • Bureaucracy • Lack of clarity and uncertainty in the administration of customs and immigration regulations	• Localize and reinforce domestic research and development efforts • Joint cooperation among domestic industry players for product development
Product upgrading	Begin to produce higher value systems that are more efficient and more affordable	• Lack of uniformed standards • Lack of innovation and research and development	• Focus on aspirational rather than currently functional products • Encourage labour market policy to offer technical training for a skilled labour force, to support growth of the sector
Chain upgrading	Use the skills developed in the solar water heating value chain to engage in the photovoltaic value chain, which is a growing and viable sector	• Lack of uniform policy across sector • Lack of investment and access to finance • Little public-private coordination • Industry maturity • Lack of training and regional expertise in newer technologies	• Inter- and intra-industry institutional partnerships • Partnerships with microfinance institutions • New opportunities to engage labour in new technical skills

(Table 6.4. continues)

Table 6.4. Upgrading Strategies, Potential Barriers and Business Model Proposals for the Solar Water Heating Industry in Barbados (*continued*)

Strategy	Steps	Barriers to Upgrading	Characteristics of a Successful Solar Water Heating Business Model
Marketing	Use innovative marketing strategies to reintroduce the domestic and regional market to solar water heaters but also to generate knowledge and interest in renewable energy products	• Lack of cultural appetite for solar and renewable energy products • Dwindling fiscal incentives for investing in solar and renewable energy products	• Rent or lease consumer agreements • Public-private sector models to create initiatives aimed at educating consumers.
Distribution and export	Increase distribution and sales of solar water heaters in the domestic, regional and extra-regional markets	• Inefficient inter-Caribbean shipping arrangements • Slow rate of construction and infrastructure development (both residential and commercial)	• Institutional partnership with maritime industry and construction sector • Establish franchises and distribution networks
Workforce development	Work with skills-based institutions to develop a cadre of workers to provide support to the sector in manufacturing, maintenance and end of product life	• Low wage rate • Statistically significant rate of voluntary unemployment	• Import parts for assembly • Profit-sharing incentive schemes

Source: Authors, based on interviews with key firms.

with companies in South America and the Caribbean would be especially lucrative in light of the Inter-American Development Bank report which points out that Latin America and the Caribbean could cover all electricity needs using renewables, including solar energy (Vergara, Alatorre and Alves 2013). Given the success of the SWH industry, the Barbados government has placed emphasis on PV production and the exploration of additional ways to harness solar energy[6] – so Barbados could potentially support a solar PV sector.

6.10.3 Fiscal Policy: Private Sector–Led Development

Government should create new fiscal policy strategies aimed at achieving specific objectives – introducing innovation and private sector–led efficiency and development in the industry. Some of these strategies might include public investment strategies, recalibrating tax and subsidy policies, and seeking appropriate levels of international development assistance.

The gradual reduction of subsidies on fossil fuels and the subsidization of green technology would redirect economic activity towards more sustainable forms of energy. The government should consider implementing a policy that provides subsidies for SWH and PV technologies. This strategy has had considerable success in a number of countries (Renner, Sweeney and Kubit 2008). However, this strategy needs to be implemented with some conditions as to industry consolidation, collaboration and innovation timelines so as not to repeat past industry mistakes.

6.10.4 Induce Domestic Market Appetite for Renewable Energy Products

Providing low-interest loans for individuals and businesses can assist the development of the SWH sector and also help create a positive market environment for avant-garde renewable energy products and PV. For example, Bangladesh's Grameen Bank has operated a loan programme for household PV systems since 1996 (Renner, Sweeney and Kubit 2008). Policymakers should also note that they cannot focus solely on the manufacturing jobs in the solar industry – there is potential for employment in the fields of incremental research and development, product design and development, installation, marketing, operations and maintenance.

Businesses might be able to benefit from fiscal dividends if tax relief options were introduced to conglomerate businesses which made smart investments in solar or renewable energy technologies. For example, an ecological tax relief policy might encourage solar technology or PV usage. Rather than merely imposing a new tax, it might make more sense to advance a shift in the focus of the taxes.

It is also recommended that policymakers institute incentives that encourage inter-industry cooperation among larger players in the sector. Such incentives may include cluster cooperation tax breaks, providing production and factory space at reduced cost, providing training for new employees, and providing grants or scholarships for research and development initiatives. The newly formed clusters should expand the scope of their operations to include PV research, manufacturing, installation and repair services, and retail.

Notes

1. There are two basic types of passive systems: the integral collector-storage passive systems and the thermosyphon systems. The integral collector-storage passive systems work best in areas where temperatures rarely fall below freezing. They also work well in households with significant daytime and evening hot-water needs. Thermosyphon systems are designed to allow water to flow through the system when warm water rises and cooler water sinks. The collector must be installed below the storage tank so that warm water will rise into the tank (US Department of Energy, http://energy.gov/energysaver/articles/solar-water-heaters, accessed 13 June 2013).
2. Glazed flat-plate collectors are used to heat water inside buildings; unglazed collectors are used to heat swimming pools.
3. Integral collector-storage systems feature one or more black tanks or tubes in an insulated, glazed box. Cold water first passes through the solar collector, which preheats the water. The water then continues on to the conventional backup water heater, providing a reliable source of hot water.
4. As discussed earlier, thermosyphon systems are designed to allow water to flow through the system when warm water rises and cool water sinks.
5. According to the Population Housing Census, there are five categories within the domestic market: chattel house, small wall house, standard wall house, wall bungalow and luxury wall bungalow (Barbados Light and Power Holdings 2012). SWH use and market penetration is highest for wall (80 per cent) and luxury wall (90 per cent) bungalows, while growth opportunities exist in chattel (10 per cent usage), small wall (20 per cent usage) and standard wall houses (50 per cent usage). The

typical SWH unit can be expected to service a washing machine, shower and dishwashing machine.
6. Several projects are already online, and the government has 37KW of PV systems installed at various sites, making it one of the leading Caribbean countries in the utilization of this technology (Gardner 2011).

References

Barbados Light and Power Holdings. 2012. *Annual Report 2012*. Bridgetown: Barbados Light and Power Holdings.

Bugler, W. 2012. "Seizing the Sunshine: Barbados' Thriving Solar Water Heater Industry". Climate and Development Knowledge Network. http://cdkn.org/wp-content/uploads/2012/09/.

Bullis, K. 2013. "Why We Need More Solar Companies to Fail". *MIT Technology Review* (March). http://www.technologyreview.com/news/512516/why-we-need-more-solar-companies-to-fail/.

Cardwell, D., and K. Bradsher. 2014. "Solar Industry Is Rebalanced by US Pressure on China". *New York Times*, 26 July.

Dalton, M. 2014. "EU Solar Firms Accuse Chinese Rivals of Violating Agreement. European Manufacturers Say LDK, JinkoSolar, Others Sell Panels Too Cheaply". June. http://online.wsj.com/articles/china-breaking-agreement-on-solar-panels-eu-makers-say-1401896061.

Gardner, D. 2011. "A Development and Implementation of a Strategy for the Promotion of Solar Water Heating in CARICOM Countries". http://cipore.org/wp-content/uploads/downloads/2013/02/Final-Report-Solar-Water-Heating-Strategy-CC-Countries-Devon-Gardner.pdf.

Gereffi, G., and K. Fernandez-Stark. 2011. *Global Value Chain Analysis: A Primer*. Durham, NC: Duke University Center on Globalization, Governance and Competitiveness. http://www.cggc.duke.edu/pdfs/2011-05-31_GVC_analysis_a_primer.pdf.

Headley, O. 2001. *Barbados Renewable Energy Scenario Current Status and Projections to 2010*. Bridgetown, Barbados: Cave Hill Centre for Resource Management and Environmental Studies.

Menanteau, P. 2007. *Policy Measures to Support Solar Water Heating: Information Incentives and Regulations*. London: World Energy Council. http://solarthermalworld.org/sites/gstec/files/WEC%20Policy%20Measures.pdf.

Navigant. 2010. *Solar Water Heating Supply Chain Market Analysis*. Milwaukee: Prepared for the City of Milwaukee and the National Renewable Energy Laboratory.

REN 21. 2012. "Renewables 2012 Global Status Report". http://www.map.ren21.net/GSR/GSR2012_low.pdf.

Renner, M., S. Sweeney and J. Kubit. 2008. *Green Jobs: Towards Sustainable Work in a Low-Carbon World*. Washington, DC: Worldwatch Institute. http://www.unep.org/PDF/UNEPGreenJobs_report08.pdf.

Vergara, W., C. Alatorre and L. Alves. 2013. "Rethinking Our Energy Future: A White Paper on Renewable Energy for the 3GFLAC Regional Energy Forum". *Discussion Paper No. IDB-DP-292*. Washington, DC: Inter-American Development Bank.